# History of
# Lumsden's Battery

From left to right, back row—Private Thrower, Orderly Sergeant George Little, Sergeant John Little, Bugler Minardo Rosser. Second row, left—Lieut. Harvey Cribbs; right, Artificer William Johnson. Front row, left—Corporal Thos. Owen, Walter Guild. Seated, on right—Sergeant James R. Maxwell; left, Rufus Jones or "Rube," T.A. Dearing's servant.

# History of
# Lumsden's Battery

Alabama Artillery in the Confederate Army
during the American Civil War

George Little

and

James R. Maxwell

**LEONAUR**

*History of*
*Lumsden's Battery*
*Alabama Artillery in the Confederate Army*
*during the American Civil War*
by George Little
and
James R. Maxwell

First published under the title
*History of*
*Lumsden's Battery*

Leonaur is an imprint
of Oakpast Ltd

Copyright in this form © 2009 Oakpast Ltd

ISBN: 978-1-84677-900-8(hardcover)
ISBN: 978-1-84677-899-5 (softcover)

**http://www.leonaur.com**

### Publisher's Notes

# Contents

This History of Lumsden's Battery
was written from memory in 1905
by Dr. Maxwell
and
Dr. Little,
with the help of a diary
kept by Dr. James T. Searcy.
From organization Nov. 4, 1861, to Oct. 15, 1863,
this data is the work of Dr. George Little,
from Oct. 15, 1863, to its surrender May 4, 1865,
the work of Mr. James R. Maxwell.

# Its Organization and Services
IN THE ARMY OF THE CONFEDERATE STATES

At the close of the spring term of the Circuit Court of Tuscaloosa County, Alabama, in May, 1861, Judge Wm. S. Mudd announced from the bench that Mr. Harvey H. Cribbs would resign the office of Sheriff of the County for the purpose of volunteering into the Army of the Confederate States and would place on the desk of the Clerk of the Court an agreement so to volunteer signed by himself, and invited all who wished to volunteer to come forward and sign the same agreement. Many of Tuscaloosa's young men signed the same day.

By the end of the week following the list had grown to about 200 men. Captain Charles L. Lumsden, a graduate of the Virginia Military Institute was commandant of Cadets at the University of Alabama and had been contemplating the getting up of a company for service in Light or Field Artillery and had been corresponding with the War Department and Army officers already in service concerning the matter.

These volunteers, on learning this fact, at once offered themselves to Captain Lumsden as a company of such artillery.

Dr. George W. Vaughn, son of Edward Bressie Vaughn (who afterwards gave two other younger sons to the cause) and Mr. Ebenezer H. Hargrove, also of Tuscaloosa County, had married two Mississippi girls, sisters, the Misses Sykes of Columbus, Mississippi, and were engaged in planting in Lowndes County, Miss. Hearing of this Artillery Co. they sent their names to be added to the list. Dr. George Little, Professor of Chemistry in Oakland College, Mississippi, and his younger brother, John Little, Principal of the Preparatory Department, resigned their places and returned to Tuscaloosa to join this Company. Edward Tarrant, Superintendent of Education for Tuscaloosa County, had a flourishing educational institute called the Columbian Institute at Taylorville four and a half miles south of Tuscaloosa. He gave up his school and joined the Company, where two of his sons, Ed William and John F., afterwards followed him.

Joseph Porter Sykes, a nephew of the Sykes sisters, had been appointed by Pres. Davis a Cadet in the regular C. S. Army and at his request was assigned to this Company. Dr. Nicholas Perkins Marlowe and Drs. Caleb and Wm. Toxey served as surgeons at different times and Dr. Jarretts and McMichael and Dr. Hill also later. We mention these doctors who entered the ranks as privates as emphasizing the spirit that was moving the young men of the time in every trade and profession. But their country had too crying a need of medical men, in a few weeks, to permit them to continue to serve with arms in their hands, and all of them were soon promoted to the service for which their education fitted them, serving as Regimental and Brigade surgeons and high in their profession after the close of the war. In May the election of officers was held and resulted in election of Charles Lumsden, Captain; George W. Vaughn, Sr., First Lieutenant; Henry H. Cribbs, Jr., First Lieutenant; Ebenezer H. Hargrove, Sr., Second Lieutenant; Edward Tarrant, Jr., Second Lieutenant; Joseph Porter Sykes, Cadet.

The following were appointed non-commissioned Officers:

George Little, Orderly Sergeant; John Snow, Quartermaster Sergeant; John A. Caldwell, Sergeant; A. Coleman Hargrove, Sergeant; Sam Hairston, Sergeant; Wiley G. W. Hester, Sergeant; Horace W. Martin, Sergeant; James L. Miller, Sergeant; Wm. B. Appling, Corporals; Wade Brooks, J. Wick Brown, James Cardwell, Thomas Owen, Alex T. Dearing, Wm. Hester, Seth Shepherd, Wm. Morris, Artificer, Wheelwright; Wm. Worduff, Artificer, Harness; C. W. Donoho, Bugler; John Drake, Farrier.

At the request of Captain Lumsden, Dr. George Little went

to Mobile and offered the service of the Company to Major General Jones M. Witters, who accepted it and promised a six gun Battery fully equipped and ordered the Company to report at once for duty at Mobile. It went down on a service steamboat and was first quartered in a cotton warehouse, Hitchock's, on Water St., and mustered into service by Captain Benjamin C. Yancy of the regular C. S. Army.

Horses and equipments were furnished and the Captain was ordered to take two 24-lb. siege guns to Hall's Mills, a turpentine still fourteen and a half miles south west of Mobile where General Gladden was encamped with a Brigade of Infantry and where a battalion of artillery was organized under the command of Major James H. Hallonquist, a West Point graduate, and when in a camp of instruction we were broken into the life and duties of soldiers, a life very different from the experience of any of the company hitherto. On March 3, 1862, the command was marched to Dog River Factory, a march of about fifteen miles, when we boarded the Steamer Dorrance and were carried to Ft. Gaines on Dauphin Island at the mouth of Mobile Bay.

At Fort Gaines the drudgery of camp life was experienced in mounting guns, blistering hands with shovels and crowbars and noses and ears by the direct rays of a semi-tropical sun.

When bounty money was paid to the command, another new experience was had by many, for released from restraints of home, church and public sentiment, it did not take long for many to learn to be quite expert gamblers. But the more thoughtful sent most of their money home to their families and parents, and the general sentiment being against such a lowering of the moral tone of the command, Captain Lumsden issued orders, absolutely forbidding all gambling in the camp, with the approval of the great majority of his men.

About this time by some unknown means, it was reported in Tuscaloosa that Captain Lumsden was intemperate or addicted to drink. As soon as the command heard of this report, they took immediate steps to "sit down on the lie," to the great relief of friends and relatives at home. Neither then nor in any succeeding years could any such charge have been truthfully made against him. The boys thought this year's service around Mobile a tough experience. They could not keep cleanly in their dress nor enjoy all luxuries of life to which they had been accustomed but the time soon came when they could look back to their first year's experience of soldier life as luxurious, in comparison to rags and semi-starvation that afterwards fell to their lot for months at a time.

Two steamboats were each making their weekly trips to Tuscaloosa and back. Parents and friends came and went. The least expression of a need, to the folks at home brought the wished for articles. Nothing was too good for the boys at the front and fish and oysters were abundant in season. The latter were in those days only considered eatable in the R. months, as the saying was: *i.e.*, during the months whose names contained the letter R. So that from May to August, the poor things could enjoy life without the fear of man. Ice was not then available to preserve them during the summer months.

At Fort Gaines, Lieutenant Cribbs was given charge of the Ordnance Department. In the early spring, the company received as recruits from Tuscaloosa many good men. Feb. 24, 1862 there arrived with Lieutenant Tarrant, James T. Searcy, John Chancellor, James Manly, Ed. King, Jno. Molette, T. Alex Dearing and ten or twelve others, E. R. Prince, Jas. F. Prince. It is from a personal diary kept by James T. Searcy that much of this first and second year's experience of the command has been culled and all of the dates.

On the trip down the boat "scraped the woods" considerably, butted out one tree by the roots, butted another that staggered the boat without injuring the tree, but left about twenty feet of the guards in the water as the tree's trophy in the encounter. Such incidents were in those days quite common in steamboat travel in low water.

Mumps, measles and kindred camp diseases made their usual inroads on the health of the command, and many of them had to spend a part of the time in the hospital in Mobile, George W.

Smith and James L. Miller among them.

Major Hallonquist was in command of the Artillery at Ft. Gaines but on April 4th was ordered to join General Bragg at Corinth, Tenn., and Colonel Melanclhan Smith took command of the Fort. Officers and men were longing to meet the enemy in battle.

At Fort Gaines, a few Yankee vessels blockading could be seen in the distance, but the monotony was wearing, and each commanding officer was pulling all possible ropes to secure orders to proceed to the front, in this case to General Albert Sidney Johnston's army near Corinth. Captain Lumsden got promises but by perhaps some political pull Gage's Mobile battery secured the deserved privilege to report at Corinth and in the battle of Shiloh got badly cut up and after the battle was ordered back to Mobile to recuperate and Lumsden's was ordered to Corinth and given the same guns and equipment.

On Sundays near Mobile Dr. Hill, a private, often officiated as a preacher so that during this first year, Sundays could be distinguished from the other days of the week. He was from near Columbus, Mississippi, and a practicing physician as well. Tuesday, April 15, 1862, three days after the battle of Shiloh, found the command at Corinth, having left Mobile on Monday and it took possession of Gage's guns, etc., on April 16th, got tents 4:00 p.m. April 17th, so for the first time for two nights, they slept on the ground in the open air, a new thing then, the general rule thereafter.

Several Tuscaloosa Doctors were near Corinth, assisting in caring for the wounded, amongst them Drs. Leland and Cochrane. Even to see so many gathered as in this first army was a new sight and experience to these raw troops.

On April 23rd the battery was attached to Chalmers Brigade, and marched twelve miles over awful roads of sticky mud and water to Monterey, where everything was next morning put in line of battle but the rifle and cannon firing was a mere reconnaissance of the enemy and all hands bivouacked in place on the wet ground.

Here much sickness prevailed and the rains were continuous. The hospital tent was soon filled and on one day Orderly Sergeant Little, out of a roll of 170 men took to a church in Corinth used as a hospital in charge of Dr. N. P. Marlowe, sixty men sick. They had measles, pneumonia, erysipelas, typhoid fever and chronic diarrhoea. At this evacuation of Corinth, the battery had barely enough men to drive the horses and General Chalmers made a detail from the 10th Mississippi infantry to fill out the company.

Want of vegetable food, drinking water from seep wells and exposure to cold rains caused the sickness. It was general in the army and probably made necessary the retreat to Tupelo when, with better water, the company and army quickly secured usual health. The evening of May 3, 1862 and that night found company under arms in line of battle with Chalmer's Brigade, but no enemy appeared. Within two weeks ending May 8th, five of the men died: Fulgham, Hall, Hyche, Sims and Lingler. They gave their lives to the cause.

To die in hospital was harder, much harder, than to die in the excitement of battle, on the field. J. T. Searcy was unable to walk from a carbuncle on his knee.

On Friday, May 9th, one section of two guns with their complement of men, having been sent forward on Monterey road, at noon opened fire on a considerable body of Yankee Infantry and a battery near Farmington. The battery replied and a considerable duel was fought. Lumsden had no causalities, but did fine shooting, as scouts reported, who passed over ground that had been occupied by the enemy, that quite a number of bodies were left by them on the field. This was the first time under fire and their action was commended by the General in command. The other section was on the Purdy road at the time, but did not get engaged.

On May 9th, Friday, two new scouts reached the battery from Tuscaloosa, Chas. J. Fiquet and John Little, the latter having given up a good position in a Mississippi College.

On the 8th a gentleman named Bozeman came to the command and proved up his son to be a minor, thus releasing him from service. The battery remained near Tupelo about two months. Lieutenant Vaughn left the battery here on sick furlough. On July 26th battery left Tupelo for Chattanooga, Tennessee marching through Columbus, Mississippi, and Tuscaloosa, Alabama. On Sunday, Aug. 3rd, at Columbus many of the command were glad of the opportunity to attend church once more, in civilized fashion, with friends and relatives of many of the command.

Nothing was too good to be lavished upon the soldier boys. Before reaching Columbus, General Bragg in passing the column noticed Lieutenant Cribb's condition; inquired about him and ordered that he report at Headquarters on reaching Columbus. When Lieutenant Cribbs did so, General Bragg furnished him one of his ambulances and ordered him to Tuscaloosa ahead, to stay until recovered. John A. Caldwell was sent with him. He was down with camp fever for some weeks and reached the battery again near Cumberland Gap, after the retreat from Kentucky.

On Friday, Aug. 8th, the Battery reached Tuscaloosa where it remained with the home people until Sunday, the 16th.

For one week, they had the freedom of the city and county, and were with their families at their own homes for the last time 'till the close of the war.

Leaving Tuscaloosa, Aug. 16th, for one week they were on the road to Chattanooga and all sorts of a time was experienced. Some "*coon* juice" "tangle-foot" was occasionally in evidence and caused some exhilaration and subsequent depression and some insubordination temporary. One good man, the Captain felt compelled to buck near Ringston, Ga., and some excitement was created among the men thereby. It is often hard for volunteers to submit to punishment of that sort even when deserved, but patriotism prevented any outbreak among the party's friends.

Sunday, August 31st, found the battery near a little town called Dunlap, the county seat of Sequatchie County, Tennessee, having been crossing the Cumberland mountains for two days.

Thence to Sparta, White County, Tennessee on Sept. 6th on an air line 40 miles from Dunlap, but much more over the Cumberland mountain route. Friday, Sept. 19th, found the battery on a hill overlooking the Federal fort at Munfordville, Kentucky, having marched from Sparta some 120 miles during the 12 preceding days. Part of time in bivouac at Red Sulphur Springs, part of the time marching, drenched to the skin for 24 hours at a stretch, passing Glasgow and Cave City.

At midnight of Tuesday the 16th, the Federal force in the front surrendered and the next day marched out and surrendered their arms, with due pomp and circumstances of war, 4200 men well clad in new uniforms of blue. Sergeant Little says, he had the night before one corn nubbin and that day a piece of pumpkin of the size of two fingers and sat on the fence eating it, while the prisoners stacked arms and thought of the 10th Satire of Juvenal and the vanity of military glory.

As our general entered the fort, he volunteered as an aid to General Bragg and passed the picket line and seeing a box of crackers on the side of the hill resigned the honorary position on the Staff and began foraging. Just as he had filled his haversack, he was halted by a sentinel and told that it was against General Bragg's orders, whereupon he desisted, but soon found another box and filled his "nose bag" with crackers and returned to the battery, giving Captain Lumsden and others a cracker apiece until all were exhausted and he then distributed a handful of crumbs to the rest of the men.

On Sept. 22nd at Hagonsville, on 23rd at Bardstown, through a land flowing with milk and honey, but themselves out of bread and living on parched corn.

There was at Bardstown a Catholic College and some of the men purchased here paper and envelopes and Dr. Little going through the library saw a volume of Humboldt's Kasmas and on telling the Librarian that he had breakfasted with Humboldt in 1858, at the home of the American Minister, Governor Wright of Indiana, at Berlin, Prussia, he told him that this was an odd volume and he could have it. While reading it the next day, seated on the top of a rail fence, he was called off suddenly by an order for the battery to move and the battle of Perryville was on, after the fight he returned to look for his book and the fence had disappeared to make a temporary breastwork and the ground was disfigured by the debris of battle.

Battery remained in camp in a beech grove for 11 days until Saturday, Oct. 4th, and surely did enjoy the rest and the hospitality of many of the citizens, who visited the camp daily. Buell's army was at Louisville and to the southwest of that city and the close proximity of the enemy, prevented much foraging at any distance from camp, for there was a liability of a call to arms at any moment. Yet some of the available supplies of the country fell to our lot, both eatable and drinkable. Frank's forge was kept busy. Vandiver told his yarns about his brother-in-law in Arkansas.

Shepard's discourses came with heavy weight through his ponderous beard. Peterson and his crowd entertained the camp with music and song describing how "*He sighed and she sighed and she sighed again and she fatched another sigh and her head dropped in.*" Billy Buck, Reuben, and Isham (Caldwell's servant) cooking biscuit and meat and pumpkins.

Charley Fiquet and others watching the cooking wistfully, a little having to go a long ways. All these remembrances of the camp near Bardstown pass in review, and then it is remembered that we had a foot deep of wheat straw, between our bodies and the wet earth, under the stretched blanket or tarpaulin. All this while the regular military duties, to care for man and beast go forward in regular routine, and all ready at a moment's notice to be rushed into line of battle at some indicated move of the enemy.

On Oct. 4th leaving vicinity of Bardstown, the battery passed through Springfield, just as citizens were leaving church on the 5th Sunday, and on the 6th passed through Perryville and on to within a mile of Harrodsburg and bivouacked for the night.

On Tuesday 7th, the command retraced its march back to within two miles of Perryville, sleeping at their guns during the night.

Next morning Lumsden's and Selden's (Montgomery, Alabama) Batteries opened the fight in a duel with two Yankee batteries, Lumsden going forward into the battle and unlimbering under fire of the enemy, losing one horse from the fourth gun.

The fighting was severe during two hours, 4:00 p.m. to dark. Sims and another man were wounded in the head by pieces of shell and Goodwyn by rifle ball. The 4th piece was dismounted and two more horses killed, then our infantry charged and drove the enemy for two miles with considerable loss to the Federals.

The battery fired about 2000 rounds, the distance being about one half mile and after the battle, the battery opposing us was seen knocked all to pieces, horses piled up and haversacks and canteens strewn over the ground, while in rear was a long line of knapsacks and overcoats laid down by the infantry before going into battle and left in their hurried retreat. Many of our men secured blue overcoats which they wore until the close of the war. Sergeant Little says he saw a thousand of them but never thought of securing any booty, but that night as it was very cold, paid a member of the company $7.00 for one which he wore until it was shot off him at Nashville.

Eventually Yankees fell back nine miles. The ground was strewed with Yankee dead, overcoats, canteens, muskets etc. Lumsden got wheels from Captain Greene to fix up the dismounted gun and remained in field until noon the next day. This was Lumsden's first battle with the whole battery. Leaving battle field about noon next day, the battery passed through Harrodsburg and on Sunday the 12th passed Camp Dick Robinson and on through Lancaster on the 13th toward Chab Orchard, the army retreating through Cumberland Gap, *via* Wild Cat, through a very poor and thinly settled country, mostly mountains. Troops lived on parched corn and beef broiled on coals without salt.

Private Kahnweiler was left sick at Munfordville, Sergeant James Cardell, at Harrodsburg. Private Wooley and Bates missing after Perryville, supposed to have been killed.

At Camp Dick Robinson, we buried some cannons in an

apple orchard inscribed with Spanish to prevent the Yankees getting them. Here were 4000 barrels of pork, that had been collected from the country and a good many barrels of whiskey, for which there was no transportation and they were burned. Bushwhackers lined the route to Cumberland Gap and it was not safe to get away from the main road.

Near Knoxville on Saturday, Oct. 25th, members of the company who had been left behind sick at commencement of the Kentucky campaign rejoined the company. Letters from home, decent clothing and more rations made the men feel better, yet still clothing was too thin for on Oct. 26th the whole army found itself covered with a blanket of snow about daylight which continued to fall the entire day. At Knoxville, Dr. Moore of the company died as also Dr. Jarrett's negro man Wash. Henry Donoho rejoined command. Ed King was left at Knoxville sick and Brown was transferred to the Ordnance Department.

Nov. 9th found battery again at Dunlap, Tenn., whence it went to Shelbyville by the 25th.

On Thursday, Nov. 27th, Sergeant Horace Martin was detailed to go to Tuscaloosa to obtain clothing for the company. Lieutenant Eb Hargrove left same day on furlough. Friday, Dec. 5th, it was snowing heavily, but the orders were received to cook two day's rations and be ready to move by 12:00 o'clock but weather proved too bad for any movement.

On Dec. 7th John F. Tarrant got his discharge for disability. Left Shelbyville on Dec. 7th, travelled pike 6 or 8 miles and bivouacked for night. A stable made quite comfortable quarters for as many as it would hold. On Monday marched through Unionville to one and a half miles from Eaglesville and camped. Friday, Dec. 20th, Eaglesville to Murfreesboro, joining again Reserve Battalion and meeting Wick Brown just arrived with three boxes of goods from Tuscaloosa, bringing something for nearly everybody.

On Dec. 28th Captain Lumsden started for Richmond, Va., sick, taking Corporal Sheperd with him. Lieutenant Cribbs was left in charge of the reserve artillery, and Lieutenant Ed Tarrant in command of the Battery.

On Dec. 30th the rifle section was ordered to report to General Breckenridge on the extreme right of the army, facing the enemy on Stone River north of Murfreesboro. The other section was in position in yard of Mr. Spence's negro quarters but was moved nearer to the enemy later in the afternoon where it remained all next day, the 31st of Dec., 1862.

# Murfreesboro

Dec. 31, 1862, most of the fighting was on the left wing when our forces drove the Federals back several miles.

The battery was first stationed on the right, near a vacated house on a hill. Here we found a barrel partly full of seconds unbolted wheat flour and a skillet and we made up some biscuit and after the first batch was cooked, the order came to move and we wrapped up the dough in a cloth and that night after crossing Stone River and throwing up some breastworks we cooked the balance on the shovels we had used for ditching.

The battery was in an open field, in front of a large brick house on a high hill where Rosecrang had massed his batteries after his right had been driven back to a right angle with its first position. This was a pivotal position and the point where the General is said to have remarked after his first day's disaster, "Bragg is a good dog, but Holdfast is better." Breckenridge made an attack on this position and as he rode into the fight, I thought him the finest looking man I had ever seen on horseback. But the position was too strong to be taken, although Bragg was in person on the field not far from us.

That night at midnight, the order came to hitch up and leave. One of the drivers reported that the horses hitched to the pole of one of the caissons, had eaten off about three feet of the seasoned oak pole. I told him to tie an extra pole under the one gnawed to a point with the halters from the horses and we marched off in retreat. The horses were almost starved as well as the men.

After going a little way on the pike, the column halted and the men marched by barefooted some of them on the frozen pike, while we built up a fire and Sergeant Hargrove, standing in front of it, had half the tail of his overcoat burned off before the warmth reached his skin.

Marching all night, we met Dr. Leland next morning, muddy as if he had been on a fox hunt in "Bear Heaven" and Jim Craddock, a noted dude, with his coat neatly buttoned and his collar clean. He was said to sleep lying on his back in a tent with ten or a dozen men, and never turned or moved lest he should disorder his clothing. But he was a brave soldier. Lieutenant Cribbs had his horse killed and several from the battery were lost here, the breastworks were nothing but rail piles from an old fence.

For three days after the two armies faced each other and on the night of Jan. 3, 1863, Bragg's army retreated.

On Jan. 4th Confederate scouts went six miles north of Murfreesboro beyond the battle field but found no enemy. Both armies had retreated. In the evening of the 4th Federals began to advance, slowly feeling their way. Corporal James T. Searcy remained a prisoner at Murfreesboro to attend to wants of his brother Reuben, fatally wounded and left in hospital. He was exchanged at City Point near Petersburg, Va., April 12, 1863, and reached the battery at Estelle Springs, Tenn., on April 20th.

The reserve artillery encamped here until spring under Major Felix H. Robertson. He kept all hands busy from early morn till dewy eve, policing camp when not engaged in drill. Evidently he believed that *Satin finds some mischief still for idle hands to do.* Friends and acquaintances from Tuscaloosa were on hand often during spring and boxes of supplies had been frequent arrivals.

May 14, 1863, on Thursday night orders came for two day's rations to be cooked up and to be ready to move by 6:00 a.m. Friday.

We moved out through Tullahoma and Roseland and camped four miles from Shelbyville and ordered to clear ground for our pack of artillery. Remained till June 5th, ordered to report to General Clayton's Brigade. Two days march in mud and rain toward Murfreesboro, was the sum total of our service with him for on Saturday night, June 6th, we were back with the Reserve Artillery again. Some of our men were great hunters and when Shuttlesworth caught an old coon with her litter of young ones, he gave a feast to his friends. Lieutenant Tarrant resigned, returned to Tuscaloosa and raised another Artillery company of which he became captain and Sette Shepherd as Lieutenant and Wm. Tarrant also.

On June 26th Battery marched to Tullahoma and was unlimbered in battery as if for a fight with 2nd section in a fort but on Tuesday, the 30th, took line of march for the Cumberland mountains through rain and mud through Alezonia to Decherd where guns and ammunition boxes were put on train wagons and carriages marched toward Sewanee or the University of the South. On July 5th, crossed Tennessee River on pontoon bridge after a weary march over hills and mountains through mud and rain. July 7th, Tuesday, Corp. Searcy was appointed Sergeant Major of Battalion thus removing him from the company.

Lieutenant Cribbs returned from Tuscaloosa on Friday night, July 10th, with a lot of supplies for the company, which he found at the foot of Lookout mountain near Chattanooga, we remained till Sept. 10th, and then were assigned to Breckenridge's Division for a week just arrived from Mississippi minus artillery. On Sept. 16th, again with Reserve near Lafayette. The two armies were on the move, manoeuvring for position, culminated in battle of Chickamauga, Sept. 20, 1863.

The whole army itching for a fight, while encamped at Tullahoma an examining board had been appointed for Artillery officers for service in the Ordnance Department consisting of Colonel Wm. Leroy Brown of the Richmond Arsenal; Colonel H. Oladowski, Chief of Ordnance of Bragg's army and Lieutenant Colonel James H. Kennard, Chief of Ordnance Officer Hardee's Corps. Orderly Sergeant Little went before this Board on Wednesday for the lieutenant's examination and on Friday for that of captain and having made the highest average in either the Army of Tennessee or that of Virginia was ordered to report for duty at the C. S. Central Laboratory at Macon, Ga., to Lieutenant Colonel John William Mallett, Superintendent of Laboratories.

He remained there until he knew the battle was imminent at Chickamauga and applied for and secured a four day's leave of absence to join Lumsden's Battery, which he learned at General Bragg's headquarters was some twenty miles distance at Lafayette. Colonel Hallonquist was then chief of artillery and offered him the command of Gaskin's battery from Brookhaven, Mississippi, whose captain was absent on sick leave.

With the consent of the lieutenants, he accepted this proposition and took charge of this battery during the battle of Chickamauga under Major General W. H. Walker who was killed at Atlanta on duty and was assigned to General Bragg's staff as assistant to the chief of Ordnance and afterwards served as ordnance officer of Clayton's Brigade, then of the Division of Cleburne, Bate, Brown Chetham, and of the corps of D. H. Hill, Breckenridge and Hardee and after a temporary command of the University of Alabama section of artillery during Wilson's raid into Alabama, closed his service with General Howell Cobb at Macon, Ga., having been in meantime assigned to duty as Chief of Ordnance Officer as Lieutenant Colonel of Artillery, of Hardee's Corps Army of Tennessee. During the battle of Chickamauga Lumsden had one private—Screniver—killed, several wounded, one gun dismounted and temporarily captured. Several men captured, among them Chas. Jerome Fiquet, Jr.

The gun was recovered next day, but was replaced by a better one captured from the enemy, with which Sept. 25th they kept up a slow fire on the enemy's breastworks at Chattanooga.

The battery was soon withdrawn from the besieging lines and joined the camp of Robertson's Battalion at the foot of Lookout mountain, reporting to General Longstreet. Here about Oct. 15, 1863, the battery received a recruit in the person of James R. Maxwell. He had since April 1, 1862, been serving as a cadet from University of Alabama Corps drill master with the 34th Alabama Regiment of Infantry, Colonel J. C. B. Mitchell but on the rolls of company C. of said Regiment as a private. He obtained a transfer and reported for duty to Captain Lumsden at this place.

Prior to this date these reminiscences have been written up from a diary kept by Sergeant Major James T. Searcy, up to July 24, 1863, date of last entry, finishing up the Tullahoma campaign of the spring of 1863 and from a few of Mr. Searcy's letters home thereafter. The succeeding pages, covering the services and camp incidents of the command are written entirely from memory by the author. Dates verified as far as possible from official records.

On being transferred to this command, I had with me a negro body servant named Jim Bobbett, taken from my father's plantation, whence he left a wife, but no children. He was allowed to come at his own request, and had been with me from the time I entered service as drill master of the 34th Alabama. There were perhaps a dozen or more servants connected with the battery, some belonging to commissioned officers, others to privates, all subject to their master's orders, but of course subject to control by the officers of the company also.

Without any legislation or orders of army commanders, such servants were part and parcel of the commands to which their owners belonged, and cheerfully did their part in connection with the commissaries of their commands, being utilized largely as company cooks. For such service they were welcomed by the commissary department and got their share of the rations, but I do not think they were ever enrolled, as a matter of record. Their masters wanted them, and the hardships of a soldier's life were very much ameliorated by them.

As a rule they were liked by all, and were glad to assist any and all soldiers for small rewards and even for personal thanks. They were great foragers, for their masters first, and next for their own and their master's friends. The officers at this time where Captain Chas. L. Lumsden and Second Lieutenant A. C. Hargrove, Lieutenant H. H. Cribbs was at home sick and soon afterwards resigned. The weather was stormy, rains came in deluges and bridges between camp and Chickamauga station were washed away, cutting off our supplies. Forage getting short, Captain Lumsden detailed perhaps twenty men to go on horses over into Wills Valley to the west of Lookout mountain.

The road to be travelled was the dirt road skirting the base of the cliff about half way up the mountain, above the Tennessee river opposite the Moccasin bend. The Federals had a battery entrenched on Moccasin Point, just across the river. The detail left before day and passed the danger point before it was light enough to be seen. By mid-day sufficient forage of corn and fodder had been obtained. Each horse and mule resembled a perambulating haystack, for it was loaded with two big sacks filled with corn on each side and as many bundles of fodder as could be tied on with ropes.

Sergeant John Little had charge of the squad, containing among others Alex Dearing, Ed King, Rufe Prince, Dave Jones and other names not remembered. It was a sort of picnic. The men bought chicken, butter and butter milk and got the farmers women to cook for them. Dave Jones bought a bee gum of honey and had a time getting out the honey, with all the crowd assisting. Then again it was good for sore eyes to loaf around in a farmer's front yard and his door steps and see his wife and daughters flitting about, and every now and then get to talk to them a little.

Calico dresses and sun bonnets perhaps, but they were a treat to the soldiers, who were tired of seeing nothing but men for so long. The detail put off having to pass the front of that battery so long as they could and had their frolic out. But they had to pass that point in daylight, in order to have time to get over the balance of that mountain road, with each animal loaded in the manner it was. There was no way of dodging it. There were rocks and woods and cuts in the road, that would protect on each side, but sight in front of the battery for perhaps forty yards or more on the road was cut out of the precipice, and for that distance it was a "*run of the gauntlet.*"

Arriving at the place, the men crowded the cut on the west side of each man on his animal made ready and as his name was called, at perhaps 30 yards interval, he made his rush as fast as he could persuade his animal to go.

The enemy could only take pot shots at one animal and not at a crowd. Those Yankees surely had sport, but they did not get to fire each of their four guns many times before all were past the bald place without the loss of man or animal. They yelled and we yelled back that they could not shoot worth "shucks." They shelled the woods along the route, but our men were out of sight and did not tarry till each reached some cover, when he halted for them to ease up, which they soon did not being able to see anything to shoot at. They had their fun target shooting. Our boys had the fun of dodging.

As there were no casualties, it could always be looked back upon, with a sportsman point of view, as one of our funny episodes. A few days thereafter camp was moved over beyond the top of Missionary Ridge, about Oct. 23rd into a woodland location, with plenty of spring and creek water nearby. To soldiers in camp a living spring was a blessing, as it was the only security against contamination and consequent disease.

Supposing the camp might turn out to be winter quarters, a long shelter was built to cover about 100 horses, with troughs made from hollow logs and racks for long forage. The men began to arrange themselves in congenial "messes" and to build pole cabins with fire places of sticks and mud plaster, and "bunks."

At the camp a lot of boxes of provisions and clothing arrived in charge of Mrs. Jane Durrett from Tuscaloosa for different Tuscaloosa boys. This good patriotic lady would leave her home and husband on a Tuscaloosa County farm and take charge of batches of supplies, provisions, clothing, etc., for officers or men. She saw to it, that every box was delivered to the soldier to whom it was sent. No man could have done this work as she did it.

Neither the pompous little lieutenant in charge of a provost guard, nor train guard, nor commanders of posts, nor the general in command of an army had any terrors for her. They were all means to be lent to the service that she was on. In the car, where her boxes went, she went, when she got with them, as far as railroad could carry her goods, her quick Irish wit and flattering tongue would soon get an order from some competent artillery for wagons and drivers and an ambulance for herself, to take her goods to their destination, and she delivered them in person to whomsoever they had been sent, officers or privates. She served one equally as heartily as the other.

Of course she had to rough it, and see much hardship and exposure, but she gloried in so serving her country. She had several sons in the army doing their duty also, as became men from such stock. Jim Bobbett, my body servant, Rube, Alex Dearing's man and some of the other company darkies had also been south on the railroad looking out for supplies.

Our messenger got a big fat gobbler, we cooked him in a big three legged cast iron wash pot. Mr. Menander Rosser reminds me that Dr. James T. Searcy, (now Superintendent of the Alabama Bryce Hospital for the Insane) was boss of that job, he put in good time for some days previous to the feast in stuffing corn meal dough down that turkey's throat, to make sure of his being good and fat at the proper time.

Can you see the picture, Searcy on a log, gobbler between his knees, left forefinger and thumb prying open the gobbler's mouth, while the balance of his left hand kept the neck straight up; right hand rolling up enormous bread pills and forcing them into the gobbler's mouth, and manipulating them down to the craw. Henry Donoho holding the bread pan assisting in rolling the pills. Several others of the mess, much interested in the operation, scattered around.

We first parboiled him till nearly tender, with an oven lid covering the pot. Then we filled him with biscuit and hard-tack crumbs and pieces of fat bacon, and cut onions and sage and the chopped gizzard and liver, all mixed; boiling down the water meanwhile to a rich gravy. Then we put the stuffed turkey in again, put on the cast oven lid heaping red hot oak and hickory coals on top and under the pot.

If the reader knows something about cooking, it is plain that this gobbler was cooked to a delightful brown, brown all over, with the juice oozing out of his skin. And that turkey was not all of that dinner.

Out of the boxes from home came material for mashed potatoes, boiled rice, cowpeas, bread and biscuit and butter, and dried peaches for a big "biled cat" for dessert with butter and brown sugar for sauce. "Biled Cat"! Eat "Biled Cat!" Yes, indeed! Soldiers thought "biled cat" good enough for anybody. Its composition was biscuit dough, rolled out into a sheet one-fourth of an inch thick, spread with stewed dried apples or peaches, seasoned with sugar and spice and everything nice, to another half inch in thickness; rolled up into a long roll and then rolled up in a clean towel or flour sack, tied up and dropped into a pot of boiling water and boiled until done.

When done the cloth unrolled and the contents cut into sections one-half an inch thick and deluged with "butter and sugar" sauce, it delightfully filled all the spaces and perhaps somewhat distended a Confederate soldier's stomach, who had already enjoyed a real good turkey and fixings dinner. What a change that was from the regular daily diet of corn pone and rancid bacon, boiled with cowpeas containing about three black weevils to the pea. As some declared most of the peas were already seasoned enough without any bacon.

At such times soldiers would live lavishly. They knew, "we are here today, where we shall be tomorrow, no one can tell." We enjoyed our good things while we could. When they were gone, we would get back to cornbread and bacon or beef hash or boiled beef as best we could, and very often the transition "was awful sudden." In winter quarters, we might be saving, and make good things last as long as possible but in intervals of a campaign, we would live whilst we could and "take no thought for the morrow."

While on the subject of "grub," who of us does not think of our efficient "boss" cook, Tom Potts? Cannot each of us see him now in this camp behind Missionary Ridge. There he sits day and night (except perhaps 9:00 or 10:00 p.m. to 3:00 a.m. when he sleeps) in his split bottom chair, in front of the centre pole of

29

his tent. Behind him his wall tent, each side piled up with boxes and barrels and sacks of meal, flour, salt, sugar, bacon, the only man in camp who always has a good tent because it is absolutely a necessity.

A tall, slouch-shouldered man, wide brim felt hat, black hair almost to his shoulders, complexion very dark, long black moustache and whiskers and eternally, when awake, a big black *meerschaum* in his mouth, puffing away. Very quiet, slow soft spon, he occasionally gives some directions about the cooking to the negroes and to the white soldiers detailed to cook. He is nothing of a hustler, but he has directed negroes from his boyhood up and is as efficient a "boss cook" as the army contained without any bluster.

Six or eight feet in front of him, a big hickory oak fire, say ten feet long, with glowing coals under the logs, skillets, ovens and pots all occupied in baking bread or boiling beef under the hands of the negro men, who delighted in the work and joke and grin and laugh or jump out and dance part of a jig, whilst another claps his hands and pats knees for the music.

Occasionally Potts may quietly say to his negro man, "Jim" I wish you would hand me a cup of water." He keeps his seat, drinks, hands back the cup and goes on smoking. No man in the army has a better coloured *meerschaum*. On the march or while the army was in the trenches, rations are issued, cooked, the bread being baked and the beef boiled, bacon or salt pork is issued raw, the soldiers eating it raw, or boiled on coals, if convenient and the meat not too scant.

In permanent camp, the soldiers drew the rations raw or cooked as they preferred almost always each mess preferred to do its own cooking. With us confederates, bread was mostly corn pone, sometimes biscuits, sometimes hard-tack. Cold cornbread or hard-tack crumbled into a tin can and boiled with perhaps a few scraps of meat was "*cush*" and "*cush*" tasted good, hot off the coals, after a hard day's march or fighting.

The writers opinion is that the word comes from Louisana where now the Creole French takes his turn of corn to mill

30

and has it ground into what the American calls "grits," but the Frenchman of Lousiana, calls it "*cous cous*."

At one time the Confederate government experimented with a mixture of cowpea flour and wheat flour, for the making of a nourishing hard tack. Doubtless it was nourishing enough, when there was plenty of time to boil them soft enough to eat, but most men's teeth were not able to grind them. It took a hatchet of ax to break them up and the broken pieces resembled shiny pieces of flint rock. They were not so great a success for the soldier on the march as the inventor expected.

Every day some of the officers and men would get permission to go to the top of the Ridge, visiting friends, in different commands, on the lines facing Chattanooga, so we kept in touch with what could be seen and heard of the situation. At the distance, the Yanks could be seen moving about in Chattanooga like ants in a hill and just about as much could be told as to what they were doing, as could be told by a man watching the doings of ants at a distance that will barely allow them to be distinguished.

Soon after our big dinner, Major Robertson ordered Captain Lumsden and one of the other batteries to be ready to march at dusk, taking only the gun detachment and guns with their carriages, leaving the caissons in camp with their horses and drivers.

These two companies were led during the night by a guide to the Tennessee River at a point a few miles above Chattanooga, with all hands warned not to speak above a whisper and to prevent all noise of movement possible and placed in position, along an open field, on top of bank of river, between midnight and day, with the information that a Federal command was just across the river in camp and only picketing confederate soldiers along our bank. So we lay, waiting for daylight, some sleeping, some chatting in whispers, in as comfortable position as the ground afforded.

Just before daylight orders were passed around to get "into battery", with cannoneers at posts and to load with shells, with fuses cut to 200 yards (point blank range) and when ordered to fire, to continue to load and fire till ordered to cease firing and move away.

Major Robertson sat his horse at a point where he had previously been in daylight, from which he knew he could get the first glimpse of the Yankee camp opposite, when it should be light enough. The other officers all on their horses in their proper positions in each battery, all drivers mounted and cannoneers at post, with guns loaded and primers stuck in the gun vents, lanyards in the hands of No. 4 cannoneer.

From across the river the Yankee bugle rang out with the "reveille", call and instantly Major Robertson's voice "Battalion! Ready! Fire!" Eight guns thundered almost as one and continued to fire each about four shots to the minute for possibly six or eight minutes, when a Federal battery replied. Then came Robertson's command, "Limber to the rear! To the right, march! Gallop!"

And away we went down the river under the cover of the sheltering woods. A piece of shell took off the arm of one of Lumsden's men, near the shoulder, as we moved away. His name was Ray, a private from somewhere in Georgia. He was attended and brought to camp in the ambulance and sent back to hospital, whether he recovered or not, we are not sure.

It developed that this little expedition was arranged the day before by Bragg's orders, as a sort of reconnaissance, to find out whether or not the Yankees had any artillery at this point, and the opposite side of the river. His order to Robertson was to leave at once if answered by artillery and not to engage in an artillery duel. All along the route of return to camp, the different commands in the trenches wanted to know what all that racket meant up the river. "We never heard guns fire so fast in our lives before." "We thought the ball must be about to open again, etc." By midday we were back in our camp again.

The battery remained in this camp till Tuesday, Nov. 24th, the morning of the battle of Missionary Ridge, when camp was broken and wagons sent to rear with all camp equipage. The fighting part was ordered to top of ridge near General Bragg's headquarters. There we remained with the battle field stretched out before us, simply ready to move, and viewing the great disaster to the confederate army to our left, we could take no part, could get to no point where needed.

Below us, in our immediate front and to our right, our men held their own manfully. Orderlies and aids galloped to headquarters, orderlies and aid galloping away again. It filtered down to us that on our extreme left, the Yankees had gained the ridge and so taking our army on its left flank. In the afternoon came orders to us, to move to the rear. We soon found ourselves travelling rearward with lots of wounded infantry and so continued till we crossed Chickamauga Creek and took a position to protect the crossing if necessary.

Here we remained until next morning Nov. 25th till 9:00 a.m., the boys finding in a deserted smoke house a barrel about half full of beef tallow. It was broken up and distributed around and came in afterwards to melt up for biscuit shortening. It tasted very well, when biscuits were eaten hot, but to be eaten cold it is not to be recommended.

Hastening to Chickamauga station, we found the torch had been applied to all the warehouses and commissary supplies that our people had been unable to move during the night.

General John Breckinridge was at the depot and ordered Captain George Little, then on his staff, to get his old Kentucky Brigade and a good battery and place them in the breastworks around the depot to protect the rear in retreat.

He found Lumsden's Battery and they remained with the Kentuckians until Sherman's troops had approached within a short distance and were about to cut them off on the east of the railroad, when General Breckinridge ordered them withdrawn to a ridge about one-half a mile to the east where General Cleburne had drawn up his division. As we crossed the railroad, shells from Sherman's battery were falling around the depot. Several women were on the station platform when the first shells hurtled past. Some dropped to their knees in prayer. The balance followed the soldiers to a barn for cover. The kneeling ones were quickly snatched to their feet and hurried away.

Despite the shelling, every passing Confederate took time to fill his haversack with hard-tack, sugar or anything that came handy and to secure as big a slab of bacon as he could find transportation for. Our gun carriers were regularly festooned with "Old Ned," as the boys called bacon. On the first hill east of the station the battery went into position, and as soon as the enemy appeared, opened on them and so continued to fire on their advancing lines until ordered to leave the position, and away we went at a gallop to the next available point and into battery again. So we continued all that afternoon, assisting the infantry rearguard of the army on that road, contesting the enemy's advance as much as possible.

When night came we continued in a slow retreat, the road being blocked with wagons and artillery and in terrible condition with mud and ruts. A mile or two per hour being the best we could do. About midnight we came to a point where another road joined ours, along which another corps had retreated, with a high ridge ahead of us to cross, mud being in many places axle deep. We had gotton half way up the hill, when the Yanks attacked the rear squad of the other corps below us. We could see the opposing rifle flashes near the foot of the hill and the minie balls were singing on all sides.

It took all the power of the teams and all the men who could get hold of each wheel to get those wagons and artillery carriages over that hill, and out of reach of the enemy while the infantry rear squad held our pursuers in check with a midnight fight in which no man could see another twenty feet away. Everybody and everything was of course coated with mud, but the Yankees got nothing for their pains.

When the pursuing forces of Osterhau's division, sustained by Hooker's Corps reached Ringgold gap, Cleburne had prepared an ambush for them and after holding them in check until night, repulsing successive charges and inflicting heavy loss on the enemy. General Hardie sent an order to Cleburne, who with

General Breckinridge and staff, were at the gap to withdraw the rear squad to Dalton, a former member of our company, by order of General Breckinridge burned the two bridges across the Chickamauga and that night the army took position at Rocky face ridge where it remained until May 6, 1864. This ended the campaign for the year as far as the reserve artillery was concerned, for when we reached Dalton, we were assigned a camp ground and at once went to work preparing quarters for the winter the date being Nov. 26, 1863.

In close proximity to a running brook and nearby springs we built log huts. Each mess was composed of individuals who associated at their own wills, without any interference of military rules or company officers. The camp was located in a nice piece of woodland, composed of oak, hickory, pine etc., on the western side of the brook or branch, from which the ground rose at a gentle slope towards the east and west, the flow being towards the north. On the eastern slope, just opposite the centre of the battalion park of artillery, Major Felix H. Robertson located his headquarters camp, with Sergeant Major James T. Searcy as his aide.

Ranged along the western slope, were the four batteries of four guns each, that composed the battalion, Lumsden's on the right, then Barrett's, Massingale's and Havis' batteries. Behind the guns of each battery were the huts of the men, about one half on each side of a wide street reaching back perhaps one hundred yards, at the head of which streets were located the quarters of the officers of the companies.

Each mess built its own hut or cabin on such plan as suited themselves and their number of individuals. The commissioned officers of each company with their negro servants built their own.

The general plan of each hut was about a 12 x 14 foot space, ground brought to a level. Two sides of 16 foot poles and back end of 14 feet were notched up at the corners to a height of about seven feet. The front end consisted of a fire place and rammed earth, with a stick and mud chimney and the doorway poles notched down on the side walls at top provided joists about 7 feet above the earthen floor, on outer ends of which joists, plates were laid to support the foot of the pole rafters. Boards of four feet in length split out from cuts of straight grained pine, made a water tight roof.

Cracks between the logs were daubed with mud which soon dried. The joists were thrown on top of them and gable ends of the same kind of boards that made the room. Bunks three or four feet wide made in two tiers were at rear end and sides bottomed with small poles, and broom-sedge and oak and pine leaves, with a blanket spread over. Four-legged slabs made good benches, but many split bottom chairs were obtained from country chair makers.

With a good log fire three or four feet long in the fire place and an old blanket hung in the doorway, soldiers were fixed to defy the coldest days of winter and sleep in comfort on the coldest nights. A good fat bed-fellow was a luxury not to be despised and on coldest nights, "spooning" was the prevailing fashion with covering well tucked under. When one wanted to turn over, it was necessary for the other to do the same. Sometimes they would do so by word of command as if at drill with "one time and two motions."

The daily military routine was "Reveille" at daybreak, stable call, breakfast, guard mounting, police of park and camp a citizen would call it, clearing up details to go out for forage and provisions. A few were allowed each day permits to go out into the country on private foraging expeditions, seeking to purchase chickens, eggs, milk, butter, buttermilk, vegetables, etc., gun squad drills, dinner, and in fine weather and good condition of the ground in afternoon often, field drill of which battery, with guns, caissons, teams, cannoneers, drivers and all stable call, supper, camp amusements of all kinds, tattoo and finally taps.

There were two buglers in the company, Charles M. Donoho was at the company headquarters. He acted as messenger also. The other, Rufus Menander Rosser was in the same mess as the writer. One of his duties was to blow the Reveille call at a certain hour each morning. His habit was to hang his bugle on the end of house plate that extended at the door. One freezing night some of the boys emptied a gourd of water into the open mouth of the bugle, thus filling the coils of same with water.

Next morning, at break of day, our friend Rosser essayed to blow "Reveille." His cheeks expand nearly to bursting, but not a note comes from the bugle, not even a part of a breath will pass through. Rosser uncovers the glowing coals amongst the ashes, pushes together the fire chunks and with his breath blows up a blaze and starts to holding bugle in same. Footsteps of boots are heard outside. They stop at our door and in pops the head of Lieutenant A. C. Hargrove with the question, "Rosser! why have you not blown Reveille?"

But his eyes take in the situation, while he asks the question, and Rosser's answer, "Lieutenant, some rascal has filled my bugle and it's full of ice," is really not needed. Off stalks the lieutenant to find Donoho, and his bugle soon sings out the familiar notes. At the end of which, each man is in ranks, front faced by the orderly sergeant who calls the company roll and then a new day's duties are begun.

Thereafter Rosser's bugle forms part of his pillow, for allowing such a mishap to occur again would mean extra work at some drudgery. The officers daily report would show up the excuses, but the boys got some little fun out of such tricks. We were all afraid of Major Robertson. His reputation was that of a harsh disciplinarian and our company was largely composed of young men of the highest social ranks. The fear was general that for some little disobedience of orders, or some infraction of military red-tape, some punishment might be ordered by him, that the culprit would rather die than submit to something degrading.

We had some object lessons. The major's hostler came to camp one night drunk. At some order of the major, the fellow let in and gave the officer a vile cursing, with opprobrious epithets, called him a half "Injin", etc., and worse still, common rumours had it that the major did have Indian blood in him and he was called generally "Comanche Robertson", but its only foundation was his unusually dark complexion and eyes.

The sergeant of the guard was sent for and the obstreperous fellow forced off to the guard house. Next morning the sergeant was ordered to bring the poor devil to the major's quarters, and hang him up by strings tied to his thumbs, with hands behind his back, till only his toes could touch the ground. So he was kept until he was almost frozen stiff. The whole command recognized the fact that the culprit deserved the severest kind of punishment. He was of a class that could not appreciate leniency and yet the men were inexpressibly shocked to see such torture.

To see a Confederate soldier subjected to brutal punishment under the very eyes of the insulted officer did not seem to be the proper thing. Had he been court-martialled and shot, it would not have shocked us half so much, but to see a white man, a volunteer serving the Confederacy subjected to a punishment that public opinion of the South would have considered brutal on even a negro slave, notwithstanding the recognized heinousness of the officer, went to our hearts.

The effect on the men in the ranks was not good, the utter helplessness of a private was brought home to us. It was hurtful to pride as Confederate soldiers serving our country for duty's sake, and fear of officers replaces badly a soldier's pride in his work. Each soldier from that time feared Robertson. Had this soldier watched his chance and murdered the officer, and then deserted to the enemy, the general opinion would have been that such action was to have been expected.

That such did not happen, showed that the disgrace was not keenly felt, by reason of the social state from which the soldier sprung, something on the New Orleans "wharf rat", order. One morning between midnight and day, one of my mess-mates was on guard at the stable lot, a mild spring morning, and the moon shining. He got tired "walking his post" so he climbed on top of the fence, under shadow of a tree and there took his seat overlooking the lot. He expected to be able easily to see or hear any inspecting officer first and to be able quietly to slide down and resume "walking his post" from under the shadow without being caught, "sitting down on a post," a disobedience of military orders always.

All at once a voice just behind him, outside the fence calls out, "Where's the sentinel here?" and there stood the major.

"Here I am, Sir!"

"Get down and walk your post, Sir!"

"All right, Sir!" But very shortly after, the corporal came from the guardhouse, with a supernumerary of the guard and relieved our friend, who was marched off to guard quarters under arrest.

Next morning he was turned over a prisoner to the charge of the succeeding guard, with a feeling of wonder hanging over him as to what sort of punishment he might expect. But he did not have to wonder long. The officer of the day came to guard quarters with instructions to give this prisoner an axe and a pick and to set him to grubbing a big pine stump in the battery park, *i.e.*, the ground occupied by the gun carriages and caissons in regulation order. My recollection is, that the stump lasted our friend several days and that it took some little help of his body servant, Rube, in the small hours of the night to get that stump out of the ground.

The grubber was busy about it during the day, and slept around the guard house fire of a night, until the stump got out of the ground. Then he was sent for to Battalion Headquarters and our major gave him quite a gentlemanly admonition, as to such "lapse from duty," etc., which was thankfully received and duly noted. Now this offense against military rules must needs have some punishment, and this punishment was received in good part, and there was no degradation in it.

Our friend took the chances, got caught and cheerfully took his medicine without a shadow of ill will against the officer ordering it. Rather he was much obliged to him for the leniency of it. It was on a par with a quite common punishment imposed on soldiers, "straggling" on a march.

One of his superior officers coming upon him a way behind his command on the road would say: "Well, what is the matter, Mr. Smith or Jones?"

"Oh! I just dropped out to get some water from a spring."

"Were you detailed? Where's your canteens?"

"No Sir! I just dropped out!"

"All right, you take a rail off that fence and bring it along, and we'll go on together."

There was no help for it. He'd have to "carry that rail." At least as long as the officer chose to stay along with him. When he wanted to ride ahead and leave the rail carrier, it would be, "Well Smith, I'll ride on, catch up soon, or I'll have to report you for straggling." Away the officer would go, down would go the rail, and Smith would probably catch up at the next resting place. Soldiers never minded such punishments inflicted in the line of military discipline. The more intelligent the private, the more he was cognizant of the necessity of discipline to an army, to prevent its disintegrating into a mob. The officer and the private might be close personal friends individually, but as soldiers, one commanded, the other obeyed.

During the winter quarters, an election was held for the junior second lieutenant, as commonly called. The two principal candidates were Orderly Sergeant John A. Caldwell, and private Robert W. Foster, both planters sons, both equally educated, and both from Tuscaloosa County. My impression is that Foster received the most votes, and he was of a most popular disposition. It is probable that Caldwell's being orderly sergeant, had lost him some votes, as no man in authority, could always please everybody, and be of any account.

Then each candidate had to stand an examination by a Board of Officers in some way, Caldwell got the commission. Foster felt much that he had been treated unfairly and wrote out an application to be transferred to the Confederate Navy. This he sent to Bragg's headquarters direct, not up through the hands of company Battalion Officials. Bragg ordered him court-martialled for this breach of military etiquette. The result was a verdict of guilty and a sentence to solitary confinement on bread and water diet for a certain number of days.

A small log hut was built close to guard quarters 10×6 feet inside, seven feet deep, without any door, the ceiling of heavy logs and roofed over, with the ordinary split boards. Foster had to climb over the wall and into the hut through a hole left in the ceiling for the purpose, logs were replaced, and roof also. His blankets of course were put in with him. His mess carried him, his big thick bread, and it was not all dough between the crusts. We do not think that water alone quenched his thirst. He had the sympathy of the whole command, who believed that his sentence was out of all reason, for a violation of military "red tape," and perhaps, treading on some one's corns.

But Lumsden saw the ill effects, threats were being made to tear the hut down, and release him; and the finest kind of soldiers were beginning to get sulky. So he mounted his horse and went to Bragg's headquarters. What transpired there none of us ever knew, but Lumsden rode back with orders for Foster's release and restoration to duty. The whole thing was a mistake, first on Bragg's part, and lastly in the sentence placed by the officers who constituted the military court.

A mere reprimand would have been ample, and not caused any sulkiness among spirited men. Forcible release of the prisoner would surely have resulted in serious consequences to many, and the possible ruining of a good command. We relate the incident as illustrating the traits of character of the two officers.

Bragg's want of tact, and Lumsden's possession of that same quality in the handling of volunteer citizen soldiers. Foster had probably more friends than ever in the whole battalion.

When not on duty, the men in camp followed their own inclinations. Books and letters and games, of all kinds. Furloughed men went home and returned for others to go. Boxes of provisions and clothing came first to one and then to another from home. Some had good musical talents, and *impromptu* concerts were of almost nightly occurrence. H. Calib Peterson, and others of like talents, contributed largely to the amusements of the

41

camp, with minstrel shows and songs with banjos, bones, reed, and other accompaniments.

One of the books that went the rounds was *St. Twelmo*, a travesty on Miss Augusta Evans, (Mrs. Wilson), St. Elmo, the heroine of St. Twelmo being described as being such a "plenary pulchritude" with attainments to suit.

At company headquarters, when the full quota of officers was on hand, were Captain C. L. Lumsden, Lieutenants Eb H. Hargrove, A. C. Hargrove, John A. Caldwell, and Cadet Lieut. Sykes. Also Chas. M. Donoho, bugler and messenger, and Henry Donoho, his cousin, headquarter's clerk. But it sometimes happened that every commissioned officer was away with Cadet Sykes, left in the command. Caldwell, being promoted to lieutenant, J. Mack Shivers, was appointed orderly sergeant. The other sergeants were John Little, James Jones, (from Autauga County,) James Cordwell and Wilds, with John Snow, quartermaster and commissary sergeant.

The corporals were: Thomas Owen, T. Alex Dearing, Wade Brook, and J. R. Maxwell, gunners, J. Wick Brown, John Watson, W. B. Appling, and ——, chiefs of caissons. About May 1st, 1864, Sherman moved out from Chattanooga, and Lumsden's Battery left winter quarters for good, never again to be in a permanent camp for any length of time.

It was placed on the left of railroad north of Dalton, on Mill creek gap at east end of Rocky face ridge.

General Joseph E. Johnston was now in command. The whole army had lost all confidence in Bragg's ability to secure the fruits of victory, gained by the hard fighting alone, of his troops. Perryville, Murfreesboro and Chickamauga had also ended.

On May 8th, the enemy attacked Stevenson's Division, along Buzzard Roost Ridge, east of railroad, and Mill Creek Gap with Geary's Division. They were easily repulsed. Lumsden's battery assisting by placing a few shells in the gap on the right of the attacking division. Geary reported a loss of 200 to 300 men, and that it was impossible to take the position by assault. As Sherman's army forged to the south west on its flanking movement, the battery was withdrawn, and on May 15th, next faced the enemy in a field of green wheat on the Oastenaula River, below the railroad bridge at Resaca, eighteen miles south of Dalton, on the day of McPherson's attack at that point, but did not get to fire a shot.

The position was on the west of a gentle rise, that inclined slightly to our rear. Had infantry charged our front, a few steps forward, would have enabled us to sweep the field. A Federal rifle battery, fired at us for a while, where we lay on the ground barely covered from their fire, when one of the shells skimmed the crest of the hill, it would miss our back a foot or two and pass on with no damage to us. The ground was hot under us, and the sun shining hot down on us, but we avoided stopping any of the shots, and we could not reach them with our smooth bores.

We lay there, with our guns loaded with canister, ready to stop an infantry charge, but it was all delivered farther to our right. Our monotony was released by chatting and munching the contents of our haversacks. We surely had a hot time there in the hot sun and shell combination, but we had no causalities. We had protection from Yankee projectiles, but none from those of Old Sol. It was McPherson's corps in our forest and south westward to success the Oastenaula. His rifle batteries commanded the railroad bridge, with pontoon and common bridge below. That night Johnston's army withdrew across the Oastenaula.

At Cassville thirty miles south of Resaca, on night of May 19th, Johnston had contemplated giving Sherman a general battle.

Orders were read to all commands announcing the battle for next day. Our men were ready, believing Johnston had Sherman's army where he could whip first one portion, then the other, but for reasons about which there is controversy, the attack of our right wing on the enemy the next morning was delayed, the opportunity was lost and the retreat continued. When we crossed the Etowah below Cartersville, the railroad bridge was burned and the battery went into position facing the crossing on a low, rocky ridge, in the afternoon.

The writer remembers, sitting down at the roots of a tree, and immediately springing up, brushing the seat of his pants vigorously. Examination showed that he had set down on a nest of little brown scorpions. Something like a crawfish in shape, with tails turned up over their backs, with a sting like a wasp's in the end of the tail. The laugh of the boys was on him.

Some Federal cavalry rode down to the river, on the other side, but a few shells scattered them, and at dark we again moved southward toward New Hope Church and Dallas.

On the afternoon of May 25th, travelling the sparsely settled country road, about 2:00 p.m. a courier brought our Captain orders to rush his guns forward, infantry and wagons giving space and away we went, the cannoneers mounting on our gun carriages and caissons. Private James Hogan, of Tuscaloosa, in attempting to mount a gun, limber in motion, fell, one wheel of the gun passing over his body. A man was ordered to stay with him and see that an ambulance carried him to a hospital. He was so injured, as to prevent him serving further during the war.

As we drew near to New Hope Church, we found infantry of Stewart's, corps, hastily building log breastworks, along the right of the road, with the rattle of heavy skirmishing in the thick forest in the front. Our battery was ordered to turn aside to the left and go into battery and wait. This threw us into position with our infantry line perhaps fifty yards in our front. The Federals attacked with Hooper's corps in force, and the battle of New Hope Church was fought and won, by our infantry line, we never getting a chance to fire a shot.

Our cannoneers lying on the ground at their posts ready to fire, should the infantry give back. At dark we were placed in position on the infantry line and ordered to intrench and by morning of 26th, we had a pretty fair earthwork in our front facing a Federal battery. The woods were very dense, and it was only a couple of hundred yards across the hollow to the Federal entrenchments. Between the two lines the earth was strewn with the Federal dead.

Both sides had skirmishers in rifle pits in front of them, and any exposure of a portion of the body brought the "ping" of a bullet in close proximity. One struck about an inch above the head of Lieutenant A. C. Hargrove, into the body of an oak against which he was sitting, a little in rear of embankment. His head showed a little too high above the breastworks. Two inches lower, it would have finished him. Both sides had to lie close in daylight. A little to the rear and left was the old church.

Captain Lumsden sent a man to General Quarles, who had his Brigade headquarters just in rear of the church, to borrow a field glass. The general and his staff wanted to know all about the situation, which was described as well as possible. One of the *aides* handed over his glasses, and requested the messenger to let them know whatever was discovered in our front. It was suggested that he come along, "Oh no! We don't think it necessary! You can tell us all about it when you return back."

The others laughed and said: "Go ahead, young man." Captain Lumsden thought he could make out a battery opposite, but it was difficult to be sure as their lines were partly hidden by brush, like our own. Our old orderly sergeant, now Captain Geo. Little, on General Bate's staff, had letters and socks from home for his two brothers, John and James, in our company, and rode up to the church where General Stewart was sitting on the steps and asked him where Lumsden's Battery was. He said "they are just over there about 100 yards, but you can't ride there, come behind the church with your horse, a man was killed where you are sitting, just now."

All was quiet then as could be. There was a country graveyard between the church and our line. He left his horse behind the church, and started to the battery, but in a moment there were a hundred bullets pattering like hail on the clap boards which covered the graves. He ran for cover in the trenches, and for ten minutes the firing was kept up and then quieted down, when he slipped back from the cover of one tree to another to the church, mounted his horse and made his way back to his own quarters.

About June 4th, the Federals disappeared from our front at New Hope Church, and we moved back and toward Lost mountain and the railroad which we crossed the next day, and on June 8th, went into position on a ridge overlooking Big Shanty Station, being on the east side of railroad. This new line came to be known as the Pine Mountain line. Here we entrenched. On June 11th, we saw a rifle battery near Big Shanty firing on our lines to the left. We fired on them. They replied. Our trenches were a little below the top of the hill, with the limber chests exposed, being higher than the works.

Lumsden ordered them to be run down close behind the works, which was done. But one Federal shell exploded one of the chests while it was being moved. Sergeant J. Mack Shivers was shoving it at the time but escaped much injury. The Yankee battery withdrew from the open, and we shortly after, heard of General Polk's death. We always believed that we were firing on the battery that killed him. During all this time we were having heavy rains every day. We have an idea that the whole army was wet to the skin every day in June.

One great trouble was to keep our corn bread dry until we could eat it. But wet bread could be turned into "hot *cush*," whenever we stopped long enough to have a fire and the weather being warm, our clothing would get moderately dry between showers. The men had by this time gotten pretty tough, and looked tough, and like a set of toughs.

Falling back on June 15th, from the Pine Mountain line, to the Kennesaw Mountain line, to face Sherman, who was flanking to our left, the battery first took position close to the top of the main spur of the mountain, a little to the right and north of the top and entrenched along with a lot of infantry. The only Federals who got within our range at this position were a lot that crowded around a railroad water tank, at the foot of the mountain. We put a few shells through the tank scattering both Yanks and water.

But the Yanks put a rifle battery off in the valley, out of our reach and went to work on us scientifically. They figured out our range and the very first shell burst about three feet exactly over our breastworks, and the next one or so killed one of our men, named Blackstock, a Georgian. A splinter clipped Horace Martin's ear—marked him. Lieutenant Hargrove was on the bare top of the mountain to see what he could see. They fired at him and the shell struck the ground in his front, and ricocheted over his head, end over end. It was certainly fine shooting and sport for those rifle gunners, and doubtless they enjoyed it. We certainly did not, but each got to a safe place and kept it, as soon as we found what those fellows could do at over a mile distance. This was on June 19th.

As this position was a worthless one for our guns, we were ordered down and moved to the south edge of Little Rinnew, relieving another battery. The change was made during the night, and Lumsden was told that it was a hot place. So we worked on the entrenchments from about midnight when we had arrived until daylight. We made good embrasures, thickened the works in our front and dug trenches for our caisson wheels close behind works, so that axles lay on the ground. The limber chests were taken from gun carriages and placed on ground close up to the works.

That afternoon, Colonel Alexander, in command of the artillery along this line, came along and Captain Lumsden told him that he'd like to find out what the enemy had over there. Colonel Alexander told Lumsden, "Well, open on them and I'll order the rifle battery further up Little Kennesaw to your right to support you." Lumsden gave him time to get up to the rifle battery, and then came his command: "Cannoneers to your posts!" Each gunner was told where to aim, and the estimated distance.

Then: "Load! Battery ready! Fire!" Those Yankees opened on our four-gun battery, with twenty-four guns and the dirt was soon flying over and around us. We fired rapidly and so did the rifle battery, but directly a shell came through Number 3 embrasure, killed Gurley, standing erect with thumb on vent, plunged into caisson just behind and exploded all three chests thereon. The flame exploded a cartridge lying on limber chest next to the breastwork and our own shell went rolling around promiscuously.

Lieutenant Hargrove grabbed a slush bucket and proceeded to pour water into the limber chest with the smashed top, where fuses were fizzling and friction primers crackling in the tray above the loaded cartridges thereon. Some of the boys yelled at him to let that thing go, but he poured that water on, and put out those fuses. Every fellow was dodging our own shells for a few minutes.

A tin strap from one of the sabots struck Corporal John Watson on the tight seat of his pants, and he dropped flat, with his hands clapped on the place where he had felt the blow, yelling: "Oh, I'm wounded, I'm wounded." The laugh was on him, when it was found that his pants were not even split.

Gracious! How those Yanks did yell, when the column of smoke went high in the air from our exploded caisson. Well, all the satisfaction we got out of the affair, was that "We found out, what the enemy had over there," and we did not stir up that hornet's nest again. Occasionally, they would plug at us, but we would lie low and not reply. One of their 24-lb. rifled parrot shells ricocheted over from the front one day without exploding.

Some of the men got it unscrewed the percussion fuse from its point and poured out a lot of powder, then dug out some more with a sharp stick, until they thought it was about empty. Then Private Dan Kelly, got hold of it, stooped down to a flat rock and jolted the point down on the rock. It struck fire, exploded and tore Kelly's arm and hand all to pieces. He was sent to hospital, then home, and I think died from the wound.

We more than evened up on the Yanks, a few days after, on June 27th, when Thomas's and McPherson's corps swarmed over their works and started for our lines in a determined assault. We filled the skirt of woods in front, full of shells until their lines appeared in the open, and then we swept the earth with canister and over their line of infantry made every bullet count, so that in our immediate front, they did not get nearer than 150 yards, and had to rush back to cover of their own entrenchments. Our command had no causalities that day, but many Federals were buried in trenches in our front, their total loss officially reported in the assault was 2,500.

Here is what is recorded in Federal official records:

> He (Sherman) Resolved: To attack the left centre of Johnston's position, and orders were given on the 24th, that on the 27th, McPherson should assault near Little Kennesaw mountain (our position,) and that Thomas should assault about a mile further south, (to our left). Kennesaw was strongly entrenched, and held by Loring's and Hardee's corps, Loring on the right, opposite McPherson and Hardee on the left opposite Thomas. About 9:00 a.m. of the 27th, the troops moved to the assault and all along the line for ten miles a furious fire of artillery and musketry was kept up. A part of Logan's 15th corps, formed in two lines, fought its way up to the slope of Little Kennesaw, carried the confederate skirmish pits and tried to go further, but was checked by the rough nature of the ground, and the fire of artillery and musketry at short range from behind breastworks. Logan's assault failed with a loss of 600 men, and his troops were withdrawn to the captured skirmish pits . . . . The assault was over by 11:30 a.m., and was a failure.

It was the most serious reverse sustained by Sherman during the campaign. The entire Union loss was nearly 2,500.

Johnston admits a Confederate loss of 808 killed and wounded. That ended Sherman's attempt to force our lines, and started his flanking operations again. Soon we were ordered back southwest of the Chattahoochee River, where we occupied a fort, overlooking the Western & Atlantic Railroad bridge, and were soon faced by the enemy with infantry and artillery again entrenched, with a rifle battery on opposite side of river three-quarters of a mile away. They would occasionally try a little target practice at our fort. Our orders were to refrain from firing unless an attempt was made to cross the river. On our side there was merely infantry enough to picket the river.

The fort was an enclosed one, *i.e.*, had parapet all around, and embrasures in all directions, as if built to stand a siege even if entirely surrounded by the enemy. Our four guns were its whole armament however, fronting the river and its destroyed bridge below us.

We here bivouacked at ease. The slope in rear of fort had some shade bushes and formed a comparatively safe camping grounds, but we lost one man here who was in rear of, and outside of the fort. A rifle shell just missed the front parapet, cut a furrow in the rear parapet, and took off the head of a private, named Maner, another Georgian. Some of us who were inside the fort saw his straw hat rise ten feet in the air and knew that another comrade had gone.

Here, on July 17th, at evening roll call, technically named the "Retreat" call, the memorable order was read to our command, relieving General Joseph E. Johnston, and placing General J. B. Hood, in command of the army. It was received in dead silence, and figuratively speaking "our hearts went down into our boots," or whatever happened to be covering our heel.

The army had still the fullest confidence in Johnston. They knew that for more than two months he had baffled Sherman in spite of his overpowering force of two to one, and had inflicted heavy losses on the enemy, with small loss to his own army either in men or material. They idolized Johnston and were ready to fight, whenever Johnston was ready. They believed "Old Joe" knew his business, and did not believe that Sherman could hold on to his line of supplies, and still surround the city. They believed that President Davis had made a terrible mistake, and that belief remains to the officers and men of the army of Tennessee to this day. They admired Hood, his personal character and gallantry, but they believed in Johnston as second only to Robert E. Lee, and that the Confederacy did not hold another man who could so well serve her.

Sherman moving the main portion of his army towards the

northeast, covered by the Chattahoochee, but still holding the W. & A. railroad with his right wing, our battery was ordered to report to General Wheeler, who with his cavalry was on the extreme right of our army. We were placed in position on the bank of the Chattahoochee, where a ravine entered the river at a very acute angle, forming a narrow ridge between river and ravine, so that by cutting down into the ground and throwing the dirt out toward the ravine, we made level places for our guns with a solid wall of earth as high as the muzzle of our guns, over-looking the slope toward the river, the hills opposite, and the Federal entrenchments along the upper edge of the fields with an embrasured battery in view. Our entrenchment, as described, made no show. We were there simply to guard against an easy crossing at this point.

Lieutenant A. C. Hargrove, next day was standing at the para-pet near muzzle of 3rd piece talking to Corporal Maxwell, who was gunner to that piece. A puff of smoke came from a Federal embrasure across the river and both squatted below the protect-ing bank. The shell struck the body of an oak tree standing just in front, and some twenty feet above the ground, tearing off a heavy fragment, slightly larger than a man's forearm, which came down with force, the end cutting through Hargroves' hat on his forehead and to the skull, a gash two inches long. Max-well said: "Lieutenant, they are cutting at us close," still looking to the front.

Hargrove said: "Well, they got me." Maxwell turned around and there stooped Hargrove, hat on ground, and his hands to his head, with blood gushing through his fingers all down over him. He was much stunned with the blow, but when Maxwell spread the lips of the wound, and the blood ran out, the solid skull of his forehead showed uncrutched. Nevertheless the blow threatened concussion of the brain, and he was sent home for several weeks. Dr. N. P. Marlowe, then surgeon with Wheeler's corps taking him in his own ambulance to the Hospital, after dressing his wound.

The enemy crossing in force, lower down the river, our battery was retired from this position and placed on the main line of defence northeast of Atlanta, and was soon faced by the enemy again, after the battle of Peachtree Creek, with his entrenchments forming quite an angle in our front, some 800 yards away, but his lines stretched from that angle almost perpendicularly away from us toward his left.

On July 22nd, Hardee's corps of Confederates attacked Sherman's left and drove it for a long distance back toward his centre. The right of this fleeing corps came into our range making for the protection of their works at this angle and Lumsden's guns shelled them just in front of their own works as they reached them, we firing over the heads of the Georgia militia, who were pushed forward across the valley as if to join in an assault, but were soon returned to their works after considerable loss.

Seeing these old citizens wounded and dying struck us with sympathy, with somewhat of the same feelings we might have experienced at seeing a lot of women sacrificed. They started in the charge, had withdrawn to the trenches again. We were accustomed to that with regular soldiers, but the sacrifice of these old citizens affected us to an unusual degree.

Being relieved from this position, by a battery attached to an infantry brigade that now occupied these trenches, we were sent to the rear and parked near a stream south of Atlanta to wash up clothing and rest a bit. But before our washing was dry, orders came to rush the battery to a position some five miles southwest of Atlanta. We went at a gallop, or trot, or walk as fast as we could rush the guns and caissons. With the cannoneers hanging on as best they could.

Reaching the position just in time, meeting our infantry slowly falling back, before the enemy, fighting as they retreated. We rushed "into battery," on a hill at edge of open field, with the Federal infantry already past the way across the field and opened on them with our usual rapid fire. In ten minutes not a Federal could be seen except the few wounded or dead left behind.

It was a terribly hot July afternoon and the men with jackets, blankets, haversacks and all else possible strewn on the ground were panting like dogs, and so wet with sweat as if just out of a river, when they threw themselves down in the shade of the trees on the edge of the field after the firing ceased with the disappearance of the enemy. We had not lost a man. Our arrival and work was so quick that the enemy rushed to the rear at once to the cover of the forest. Our guns used some 33 or 34 rounds each in the short time in action.

All night infantry and artillery men worked with every available tool, down to the bayonet to loosen up the earth, and half of a split canteen to throw up the dirt and next morning found us entrenched in our new line. But on the other edge of the field, the Yankee trenches showed up some 800 yards away.

In this position Lumsden's Battery remained nearly all the month of August. Every few days we would have an artillery duel with the rifle battery opposite. Sherman was now extending his right wing, which finally led to the assault of Love Joy station, on the road south of Atlanta. He had also brought down siege guns, that fired shells about the size of nail keg, and was shelling the city. One Sunday we had a particularly fierce duel with our opponents. It happened that the embrasure of the 3rd piece flared a little more squarely to the front of the others. Three whole shells struck the 3rd gun during the action, each coming through the embrasure only about one foot in width.

One struck on top between trunnions and vent, gouging out the brass like a half round chisel would have gouged a piece of wood, and glanced on to the rear. The second struck gun carriage on left cheek, just in front of left trunnion and went into small fragments in every direction. The third struck the edge of the muzzle, and crushed it so that we could get no more shells into the gun. It was ruined temporarily, and had to be sent to the arsenal at Macon.

About this time, General Hardee and staff rode up. He inquired: "What's the matter here?"

"Nothing," said Lumsden, "but those fellows opened on us and I make it a point to give as good as they send."

"Well, cease firing its doing no good, and we must husband

our ammunition."

Old man Lane had the front end of one foot cut off by a piece of shell. He was bringing up an armful of cartridges from the caissons under the hill at the time, but did not throw down his load until he brought it to the gun, loudly proclaiming, that he hoped these shells would pay them back for his wound. But that was the end of his service in our army. He was over con-script age, but came as a substitute for someone who could pay for a man to take his place.

I believe that he was the only man struck that day in our company, but in rear of the 3rd gun that had been put out of action, a bunch of canteens, hanging on a forked post were all rendered useless by pieces of shell or bullets coming through the embrasure. The Yankee three-inch rifle was a dead shot at any distance under a mile. They could hit the head of a flour barrel more often than miss, unless the gunner got rattled. The shell consisted of three parts, a conical head with smaller cylinderical base, a cap to fit, that base loosely and a ring of lead that con-nected the head and base.

When fired the cap at butt was thrown forward on the cyl-inderical base of the cone, expanding the lead ring into the grooves of the rifle, the cone exploding by percussion cap on striking. It was the most accurate field piece of that date. Our smooth bore 12 pounders were always at a disadvantage in ar-tillery duels, but with time fuses and at masses of men, or at a battery in open field, 800 to 1,000 yards, they did good service, and with canisters they could sweep the earth.

After Lovejoy's station, we were moved up to the city, and put into a casemated fort for a short time in the outskirts of the city, whilst evacuation was going on, and were among the last of the commands to leave the doomed town, whence we retreated with a portion of the infantry toward Macon, Ga. Burning stores of all kinds were located by the soldiers, mail cars sacked, and letters and packages of all kinds gone through at road side fires in search of money, the useless letters feeding the fire. This was on the night of September 2, 1864. Rations on the retreat got very short and for once our men were forced to live off the country. When bivouac was made for the night above Macon, for the success of our own particular mess, all scattered after "retreat" roll call in different directions. About midnight they had all come in, and pots, kettles, ovens, and hot coals were in demand. Henry Donoho had shelled out about a peck of cornfield beans from the nearly ripe pods in the fields.

Walter Guild turned up with a long stick across his shoulder, with two large pumpkins stuck on each end. Ed King and Jim Maxwell each had a sack of sweet potatoes, grabbled in a field a mile and a half away.

The Rosser boys had corn too hard for roasting, but all right to grate on an old half canteen grater.

Rube, Aleck Dearing's servant had half a shoat and Jim Bobbett, my own servant, had two ducks.

Someone owned a big brass kettle, that would hold about half a barrel, which the wagons hauled, and it was soon on the fire, filled with the sliced pumpkins, to be stewed down. Some did one thing, and some another, and by an hour before day, that feast was ready, and several more along the same lines in the camp. We ate our fill, filled haversacks, distributed the balance to whoever wanted it and were ready to move at daylight. I believe that it was the only meal I remember during the war, where everything was the proceeds of plunder.

We had been pretty close to a famine for a day or two, but this was surely a feast.

It was all contrary to military law, but soldiers were not going to sit still and starve, when something to eat could be had out of the fields for the taking, and the officers could not be expected to sit up nights to come around and inspect our pots and kettles, and if they did, they could prove nothing, and so, for the occasion and the recognizing necessity, nothing was ever said about it. The men were on hand ready and able to do duty, and the tangle of the crisis was soon straightened out and our rations coming through the regular channels.

From Macon, by way of Griffin, where a few days were spent

in camp and thence to West Point on the Georgia-Alabama line, where preparations were made to cut loose from the railroad, and traverse northeast Alabama with Hood's army to strike for middle Tennessee by way of Decatur and Florence, west of the mountains. This was now ———, so that we had been months and days in reaching in a roundabout manner since the fall of Atlanta, on Sept. 2. Hood's infantry and cavalry had been some-where south, and southwest of Atlanta. Sherman was fixing to destroy, and strike out southeast across Georgia, and Hood was preparing to strike out for middle Tennessee and Nashville.

With our guns and wagons, we joined the army wagon train, making its way northwestward, during a very rainy spell of weather. Travelling through the flat piney woods was awful. The white loblolly mud was often axle deep in the road, and turning out in these flats did not seem to better the matter much.

The writer had now been appointed a sergeant, and been given a pie bald pony to ride at the head of his 4th Detachment of gun caisson. One day his pony got both feet on same side into a deep rut under the loblolly and down flat broadside he went and the writer disappeared. When he emerged he was greeted with the well known yell, "Come out of that, I see your ears sticking out." When the mud dried, it flaked off and I was not much worse off temporarily than the balance of the crowd and they were welcome to the fun.

Finally, we reached the Tennessee Valley, in Morgan County, and marched westward. The sites of the old plantation homes were now marked only by groups of chimneys, the plantations a dreary waste. Reaching vicinity of Decatur about ——— we found it garrisoned by a Federal force with entrenchments, but Hood's objective point for crossing the Tennessee River was between Tuscumbia and Florence. Near Tuscumbia, our battery was again in camp for a few days.

As from West Point to Florence in a direct line is about 200 miles by the route travelled by us 250 or 275 miles of continu-ous march. We were not sorry to get a chance to rest, wash, clean and repair up. Here, in the garden spot of Alabama, prior to the war, food was scarce. The beef issued to us could not produce a bead of fat, on the top of the pot, when boiled. Bacon or salt pork, when we got any was generally rancid. But we got here one unusual luxury in the way of food, a fine young fat mule had its back broken by the fall of a tree, cut down in camp. So it was killed and the boys took possession and divided it out.

It was very fat. The fat from its "innards" was "tryed" out like oil and saved in bottles and cans for "breadshortening" for which it answered well. The meat was very fine, much better than any beef we had gotton for a long time. But the boys made all sorts of fun over it. We had some left to carry along on the march, and a soldier would pull out a hunk from his haversack, throw up his head and let out a big mule bray, "a-h-h-h u-n-k, a-h-h-h u-n-k, a-h-h-h u-n-k," bite off a mouthfull and go to chewing.

The crossing of the Tennessee on the night of Nov. 20, 1864, over a pontoon bridge at south Florence was to officers and men of Lumsden's Battery only one of many disagreeable experiences. No more than our whole army had gotton used to experiencing in such campaigns in all sorts of weather and conditions, its locality merely makes it stand out in the memory, a little more prominently than other such experiences. Notified in the afternoon to be ready in our turn to cross over, then again to fall into the line on the South bank after dusk; moving on to the bridge after dark, and occupying several hours in crossing, moving a few paces in the bridge, then halting and standing shivering in a drizzling rain, until again a few paces could be gained.

Then at the north bank, getting our teams up the steep banks through mud axle deep, by doubling teams and all hands at the wheels and getting through the night, hovering over roadside fires along streets of Florence and roads beyond until daylight brought a possibility of finding a place to make a temporary halt for feed and rest for man and beast.

On November 27th, reaching the vicinity of Columbia, where Schofield was entrenched with an army of about the same size as Hood's, a demonstration was made of an attack on his lines, but the main position of our army crossed Duck River above Columbia and struck for Spring Hill on the turn pike between Columbia and Franklin.

On 29th, the Battalion of Reserve Artillery was ordered to leave guns and caissons, with horses and drivers, under charge of one commissioned officer south of Duck River. The captains, two lieutenants, non–commissioned officers and cannoneers were ordered to follow the infantry brigades; the object being to be able to man any batteries that might be captured from the enemy in this move against his rear. Lumsden was ordered to report to Brigadier General Reynolds and to keep right up with his brigade under all circumstances.

It was nearly dark when we found ourselves in a half mile of Spring Hill, and there, we remained all night, without any attack being delivered on the enemy hurrying northward along the pike, wagons, artillery and all other vehicles kept on a rush with their infantry on east side of the pike to protect against our attack.

Time was lost during the day in building rough bridges across creeks waist deep to infantry, which had better have been waded, for the few hours so lost, prevented a successful attack at Spring Hill which Hood had planned to demolish Schofield.

Forrest was trying to delay their advance toward Franklin, and sometimes succeeded in getting possession of pike for a short time, capturing teamsters shooting down teams in their harness and setting fire to their wagons.

But their rear passed Spring Hill before daylight the next morning, with Hood's infantry pursuing their rearguard closely into Franklin, where a strong line of entrenchments had been prepared around the edge of the city from Harpeth River above the same below town, and a strong line of rifle pits out in front of the regular trenches.

On the afternoon of Nov. 30, 1864, Hood attacked these entrenchments about 4:00 p.m. Reynolds' brigade was on the right of the pike, somewhat to the right of the historic genhouse. As this brigade started in the charge on the first line of rifle pits, Lumsden's command was close behind with no weapons but their bare hands. General Reynolds noticed it and riding up called out to Captain Lumsden: "Captain, take your men back behind the hill to our rear."

And so it was done; though as soon as our infantry reached the valley and the bullets ceased to fly so thickly about the top of the hill, the whole company was soon at the top of the ridge, watching the terrible struggle in our front over the Federal entrenchments on the outskirts of Franklin.

Away in the night, the flashing rifles revealed the firing of two armies with a bank of six feet of earth between them, until finally it gradually ceased. Before daylight we got certain intelligence that the enemy was gone through Corporal Tom Owen, gunner to 2nd piece, who with another prospecting companion or two had been into the town and returned with a bucket of molasses and some other eatables.

Here we were left by General Reynolds' brigade, and where our horses, guns and caissons came up, Lumsden's Battery was again in its usual fighting trim, and moved on to Nashville where it was on Dec. 4th, in the front trenches on the left of the Grannary White Pike, in the yard of a fine brick house, which the enemy had destroyed just outside of their fortifications, known as the "Gales house".

Our lines were so close to those of the enemy across a narrow valley of cleared fields, that no one could expose any portion of his body on either work, without drawing the fire of his enemy opposite. Some of the boys found good quarters inside of the old furnace, within a few steps of our guns, those of us in the outside wishing there were a few more furnaces. Talk about not dodging! Whenever one of us had to move about, he had to dodge from one cover to another. But there was one comfort, our infantry kept our enemies dodging also.

About Dec. 10th, we were relieved from this position by another battery, and ordered to the extreme left of the army and put in position on a small hill, about 700 yards west of the

Hillsboro pike, opposite the house of Robert Castleman, who lived on the east side of said pike some three and a half miles south of Nashville, and three quarters of a mile, southwest from the extreme western end of Hood's line, on the Hillsboro pike. Here, we were ordered to entrench.

Major John Foster of the Engineers, with a detail of 100 men had already started on the work. Hood's orders were that it should be a regular fort enclosing the top of hill. As yet, it was simply a redoubt, facing a ridge some 800 yards away that ran nearly perpendicularly to the general direction of the army's line of battle at the extreme left end of the army. Between the ridge and the location of redoubt were cultivated fields, and had been some woods, through which Richland Creek meandered towards the north west.

The woods our engineers had cut down, so as to give an uninterrupted view of the lands in our front, and gave a cover for skirmishers who might be driven back towards redoubt and also gave cover for an enemy line of skirmishers to approach to within 100 yards of redoubt under cover, when they had driven back the defending skirmishers.

Major Foster's force had started the redoubt shortly after the remnant of Hood's Army (after Franklin) had aligned itself before Nashville and entrenched somewhere about December 1st to 3rd, it being perhaps a mile or more from extreme left of Hood's army to the Cumberland River. General Chalmers with Cavalry, and the remnant of Ector's Brigade of infantry as a support, guarding the gaps between left of Hood's entrenchments at Hillsboro Pike, to Cumberland River. From the date of our arrival at fort location we had rain snow, and sleet, and the ground frozen hard, so that it was impossible to make any rapid progress on the redoubt laid off for four embrasures for our four Napoleon guns.

Stretched blankets and the tarpaulins from for our guns and ammunition were the only cover for officers or men. I well remember that, the day before the battle of the 15th, my servant Jim Bobbett brought me a change of clean under clothing, for which I had to scrape off the snow on a log at Richland Creek, strip and bathe in its icy waters to make a change.

By the 15th (the day of the battle) we had manerals so long. At my gun we had lost Private Horton and Corporal Gunner Ed. King. Hilen L. Rosser at another gun had part of his head shot away. That night as I was pouring some water for Lumsden to wash, he was picking something out of his beard, and said: "Maxwell, that is part of Rosser's brains", out of the 40 men that we had at guns, we had only twenty-two left, balance having been killed or captured. A Federal officer rode around Lieutenant A. C. Hargrove and demanded his surrender, and cut down at his head with his sabre. Hargrove caught the blow on his arm, but it beat down his arm to his head enough to "hurt like thunder", as Hargrove expressed it.

Hargrove grabbed a loose tree branch and struck at Yank's horse which about that time got a bullet from our infantry line and ran away from Hargrove, so that he made it to our new line.

That night we buried Horton near the Franklin Pike, where we bivouacked. I cut his name on a headboard, and command to which he belonged.

A detail was sent to the house that had been used as a hospital to bring his body. A long, tall, red-headed private, John Walker, was one of that detail. He had been carrying a great long navy revolver for months for use in such circumstances. When asked how many times he shot it. He laughed and said it was as much as he could do to persuade himself that he was able to get out with it.

It was about 12 o'clock that Captain Lumsden sent orderly Sergeant J. Mack Shivers on horseback to report to General Stewart that all Confederate infantry had been driven into the fallen timber at our front, and that it was evident the enemy would soon rush us with a charge. That we could leave the guns and get away with all the men.

Shivers returned with the orders, "Tell Captain Lumsden it is necessary to hold the enemy in check to the last minute regardless of losses." This was about 12:30 p.m. They overwhelmed us about 2 p.m.

So that Lumsden's Battery alone had stopped the advance of A. J. Smith's Federal Corps for three hours during which Confederate troops had been moved from right wing to a new line behind the Hillsboro Pike several hundred yards in our rear, which was all important, to the Confederates.

Moving southward from Nashville battlefield, with the remnant of Hood's army, Lumsden's Battery was now but a name for a command of men without arms, with a quota of horses, wagons for commissary and quartermaster's supplies with their drivers, one half its cannoneers having been lost at Nashville, killed wounded and prisoners.

A relation of a few happenings along this dreary march in midwinter the roads, a loblolly of sleet and turnpike dust and grit, may serve to show how Lumsden and his officers maintained discipline without resort to severe or degrading punishment for lapses from duty. Like all volunteer commands, it had in its ranks men from all conditions of life and of various degrees of education from the collegiate down to the illiterate man who could not write his own name. But perhaps one half of the enlisted men or privates were graduates and had started into professional life or had left college to give their services to their country before the end of the university terms.

They were gentlemen, and imbued generally with the high sense of honour and devotion to duty usual among boys and men in such social standing. They gave the general tone to the command and the officers were careful to do all possible to keep its moral tone and to impose no punishment that would lower the culprit in his own estimation. They did punish by imposing extra duties for violation of military rules, but always the individual punished as well as all his comrades were perfectly conscious that the punishment was deserved, and therefore necessary.

For instance a private had been grumbling for several weeks to his sergeant about putting him on details so often, ignoring the fact that the numerous jobs to be attended to, brought around often to each man, his time to go on detail. One morning this private said something to the sergeant who was at the time cutting up the detachment's cooked beef into equal portions, that passed the sergeant's patience. He laid down his knife, got up and faced the man, with the remark: "I've stood your jaw as long as I intend to", and delivered him a blow with his fist between the eyes. Of course things were lively for a while until Lieutenant Hargrove ran up interfered forcibly between the combatants and ordered them back to the duties on hand.

Some nights after the sergeant was standing by the Captain's fire and no one was near, but Captain Lumsden, who said: "What was the matter with you and ——, the other morning?"

"Nothing much, Captain, except he had been grumbling and fussing for some time, whenever his time came to be detailed on a job, and just got so I could not stand it any longer, and determined to put a stop to it."

"Well, you've no right to strike any of these men with your fist. If a man is insubordinate, you have a right to shoot him, but not to strike him with your fist."

The sergeant laughed and replied: "But it was not bad enough for that, and of course I was not going to shoot him, but I don't think he will need any more."

There was never anything more said about it, and the soldier quit grumbling and did his part thereafter, as well as anyone to the end of the war. Another case in point, just after leaving Nashville, a non-commissioned officer had been affected with boils, so that he could not ride horseback for a few days, and it was against orders to ride in the wagons. His boots were split at the counters, the soles were tied to the uppers by strings and he had no socks.

The turnpike gritty freezing slush worked into his feet until he could hardly hobble, so he would watch his chance, when no officers eye was on him, and crawl into a wagon and there stay until camp was reached at night when he would crawl out. One night, when he crawled out in a drizzling cold rain, and finding a fire in an old barn on the opposite side of the road, with soldiers of another command, he remained there in comparative comfort all night, and after daylight turned up at the officers fire. Lieutenant A. C. Hargrove said to him: "Where were you last night, Sir, after we went into camp?"

"I slept in that barn across the road."

"Well, we had to send a detail with horses back to the pontoon train, and I wanted to send you in charge of it, but no one could find you anywhere. You have been straggling ever since we left Nashville, and not attending to your duties."

"Lieutenant, I've not been straggling, as you think I have. Look at my feet, I could not walk and keep up. I had boils so that I could not ride my horse. The only way I could keep up was to steal rides in a wagon during the day, and that's what I have been doing."

"Well, you have not been excused by the surgeon."

"No, Sir, I did not want to be sent away from the command." When the lieutenant. walked off, the captain said: "I'll tell you what's the matter with you. You've got out of heart. You've lost all hope of our winning this fight. It does look black. But the thing for you and me and all the balance of us to do, is to just stand it out to the end. It can't last much longer. That is true. But when it is done, we all of us want to be conscious that we have done our duty from start to finish."

"Captain, I've always done all I was able to do, and expect to, until the end comes."

"That is true and, we'll hold out to the end."

That was Lumsden's way of controlling his men. He made them feel as if he knew that it was their determination to do their full duty, and the whole tone of the battery was kept up to the standard by the idea. The high standard of its *personale* was the result not of fear or compulsion, but of individual personal patriotism.

On this retreat it was difficult to find food for the army, and first one command, then another, ran mighty short. Passing through a mountainous thinly settled country during Christmas week, our captain gave a few permits to different individuals to forage off the line of march. One forager heard of some mills along a creek some miles off the line of retreat, and struck out for them horseback. On his arrival at the first, he found it crowded with infantry men, each guarding his sack of wheat, and awaiting his turn to run it through the mill. The miller was there, and was asked if he could sell a sack of wheat. He replied: "these soldiers say they are bound to have all there is, and I help them grind it, to save injury to my mill. The wheat belongs to the neighbourhood."

"Where is there another mill?"

"About three miles down the creek."

Off our forager rode. He saw that money nor begging would prevail to get bread and determined on a bluff. The next mill had soldiers claiming all the wheat, but some of it was in boxes or bins. He called the miller out, and offered to pay for a couple of bushels. "It is not mine, said the miller, it belongs to people around here, but I had better take even Confederate money for it, than nothing at all, and if you can get a couple of bushels, go ahead."

So into the mill our man went, with his sack, and walked up to a box holding perhaps ten bushels, on which sat a soldier with his rifle leaning against the box, with the request: "Let me get at the box, if you please."

"You can't get any of this meal, our men need it all", reaching for his gun.

"I'll show you about that, Sir, my men have had no bread for three days, and some of this wheat, I'm going to have" and he began shovelling it into his sack, regardless of protests, until sack was full; then he said, "that is all I want," turned to the mill hopper dumped it in, as soon as the same was about empty, putting his sack under the spout. When his sack was full of whole wheat meal, he tied it, paid the miller and rode off rejoicing. When he found the command that night, some hogs had been brought and issued by the commissary, and the two bushels of wheat meal was a Godsend. Our mess, after breakfast next morning, divided out to each, eleven big army biscuits apiece, but before dinner time, one gaunt member of the mess had finished up his lot and was on the lookout for more.

Recrossing the Tennessee River on the —— day of December near Brainbridge, we camped a few days near Tuka, Mississippi, for rest and a general cleaning up, but many soldiers had no clothing except the ragged suits they had on, and cleaning involved the washing and drying of a portion of their garments at a time.

A Confederate private at that time could be pictured in words about thus: A pair of old shoes or boots, with soles gaping, and tied to the uppers with strings, no socks, threadbare pants, patched at the knees, burnt out at the bottom behind, half way to his knees, his back calves black with smoke, from standing with his back to fires, his shirt sticking out of holes in rear of his pants, a weather beaten jeans jacket out at elbows and collar greasy, and an old slouch wool hat hanging about his face, with a tuft of hair sticking out at the crown.

The officers, in many cases, did not show up much better. In either case, the man, who had a negro body servant along, fared the best, and was kept clothed the best.

The negro slaves usually had money in their pockets, when their masters had none, that they made serving officers and men in many ways.

The writer's own servant, Jim Bobbett by name, had left his wife on my father's plantation in Tuscaloosa County, Alabama, but had no children. He was selected from several who desired the place, as being a handy fellow all round. A pure negro, with flat nose, and merry disposition. From mere love of myself and a determination to see that I should never lack food or clothing, as long as he could obtain the wherewithal to prevent it, he was faithful in that service, just as a Confederate soldier was faithful in the service of the government he was fighting for.

He wore a broad flat waterproof belt next to his skin, and scarcely ever had less than $100.00 therein, and often as high as $1,000.00. He was a good barber and clothes cleaner, and a handy man in many ways, and a few weeks stop of the army in camp soon replenished his "bank" and out of it he generally procured what was needed for me or himself or his friends, without any interference or direction from me.

If he got more than he needed, he disposed of his surplus at a profit. I suppose that if neither a slick tongue nor money would procure necessities, he did not hesitate to "press" them. But his jolly flattering tongue, with the women of his race, along our routes made him their favourite, and when he bade them "goodbye" his "grub" bucket would be filled with the best to be had. When he and his pals were behind, when the wagon train came up, we did not kick, but would turn in, perhaps supperless, to sleep, knowing that some time before day, they would arrive with something to fill us up.

I suppose that some of his class did desert to the enemy, but the large majority were true as steel to their masters and their duty, from the beginning to the end, often at great personal risk and none attached to our company ever deserted. They could have done so easily at any time, and been free inside of the enemies' lines, but personal loyalty to their masters and their own people, as they considered their master's families held them cheerfully to their duty. There was no compulsion about it. They struggled and foraged and speculated at their own sweet will, yet all the time, looking out for their master's interests over and above all else.

These facts are some of the strongest proofs, that between masters and slaves of those old days, there were ties as strong as steel, in the close personal relationship that neither forgot. It had its counterpart in the love and service of the old "Mammy" to her master's family and children. She loved them, and delighted to serve and care for them, sometimes to the neglect of her own flesh and blood.

One morning in bivouac, near Tuka, at breakfast, around the officers fire, there was served a fine skillet full of fried pigeons, with gravy and biscuit, washed down with burnt corn coffee. Old "Ike," Lieutenant Caldwell's darky had come in during the night from a forage, Lieutenant Hargrove with the others of the mess, was enjoying the meal when all at once, Hargrove says: "Ike, where did you get these pigeons?"

"Oh! Marse Cole, don't you bodded about dat. You eat your breakfast."

"Ike, you old rascal, I believe you stole these pigeons, and if I had anything else to eat, I wouldn't eat them."

"Dar now, Marse Cole, it's a blessed thing, dat you'se got me and dese udder fellows to look atter dis mess, kaze if it twant for us, you'd go hungry many a time, and dats a fac."

"Well," said another officer, "its a bully old breakfast anyhow, and we don't know when we'll get such another."

From Tuka, the command with its wagons marched to Columbus, Mississippi, where it went into camp near the outskirts of the town. Here, there came down from Corinth, Aleck Dearing and John Bartee, who having been on sick furlough in Tuscaloosa, had missed the Tennessee campaign, with them were some others and also some conscripts among whom was Richard Maxwell, the youngest of the old firm of T. J. R. & R. Maxwell, who had to at last take the field, having served some time in Leach & Avery's hat factory and thus exempt for that time from conscription.

This squad of returning men, had charge of boxes of clothing for most of the men in the command and provisions furnished by friends and relatives in Tuscaloosa, which they had gotten up to Corinth with it trying to reach Hood's army, wherever it might be. At Corinth some quartermaster had furnished them a wall tent with "fly" to protect the goods. When ordered to move with the goods from Corinth, down to Columbus, by train, they were ordered to return the tent and fly. But they were too experienced old soldiers for that, so they hustled boxes, tent and all to the train, and came on to Columbus, with the whole lay out.

They made a present of the fly to the officers of the company, and kept the tent to protect the goods until distributed, and incidently themselves. This tent and fly were the only ones left in the company now, as nothing of the kind had been on hand for many a month.

During rains, a blanket stretched over a pole, three feet from the ground, would somewhat shelter three men. When it was not raining, shelter was unnecessary to the hard old veterans.

Once again and for the last time, Lumsden and most of his men got into whole and comfortable clothing. Our new comrade, Richard Maxwell did not hold out long. He had lately married a young wife, and nostalgia got hold of him, he lost all appetite, and was attacked with dysentery, so off he was sent to hospital in Columbus. There he did not improve, and he persuaded the surgeon in charge to order him to report to Tuscaloosa hospital. He soon found friends in Columbus to take him home.

The most of Hood's army, that still had arms, were now rushed around by rail, *via* Meridian, Selma, Montgomery, West Point, Macon and on to North Carolina to General Jos. E. Johnston, once more to try to prevent Sherman's march to the rear of Richmond. Our command having no guns was ordered to report to General Dabney H. Maury, at Mobile, the old drivers now to act as cannoneers, making up sufficient to again man a four or six gun battery in a fort.

At Mobile we were placed temporarily at Battery B., above Mobile in a fort with big cast iron siege guns, commanding a portion of the march. We were soon well drilled in the handling of siege artillery of this class, and also had some practice with small Coehorn mortars, firing at targets out in the marsh. Here, the boys went in for a good time whenever they could get permits to visit down in the city. They would test the restaurants to see what sort of meals Confederate money would still bring in a big city on the sea coast.

Fish and oysters were plentiful, as well as eggs and vegetables. But for coffee we had to take whatever substitute was available. Usually sweet potatoes, okra or sage. For sweetening either long sweetening (molasses) or short sweetening (a moist clammy dark brown sugar.) For cream, if wanted, a beaten egg answered, but most of us preferred the "coffee" "barefooted and baldheaded," *i.e.*, without cream or sugar, or "straight." Some little new corn whiskey, white as water, could be had also "*sub rosa*." Occasionally, at a social call at some private residence, home-made wine from grapes or blackberry might be set before the caller, but real coffee or tea, or white sugar was hardly to be had, for love or money.

One night in company with a mess mate we got permission to go to the city to call on friends. These friends were the family of a commission merchant, who was a friend of our parents, and included an eldest daughter who was quite a noted authoress, extremely well read and learned, and two younger daughters. We found several high officers were also callers, rigged out in their best uniforms, with their proper insignia of rank in golden stars and lacing. We were in our new gray jeans jackets and pants and linsey shirts, lately gotton from home at Columbus. But that did not make any difference at all. We were welcomed, introduced all around, entertained on an equality. In fact one of the higher officers we found to be an old college mate.

The officers from generals to captains were of course older than we, who were each only about twenty years of age, so that naturally they fell to the older members of the family, while we were entertained by the younger daughters, who were in their "teens." With back gammon checkers and cards the evening passed pleasantly. When we boys, who had to foot it two or three miles, made our *adieux*, the ladies accompanied us to the door, asked us to call on them again and the authoress said, as we were about to leave the door: "I hope you gentlemen will not form an opinion about the meteorology of Mobile, by what you have seen since your arrival."

My friend said: "Yes, Madam," and we both bade them all goodnight.

As we walked up the street, my friend said: "Jim, what in the mischief was that she said? Meteor-meteor, what?"

"Oh" I said: "She meant she hoped we would not think they had this sort of weather here, all the time."

"Oh, shucks; I could not make it out."

A few days after, General Maury held a review of his army on Government Street. We were ordered in. We had in our company, several soldiers, who had neither coat nor pants. They were down to shirts and drawers, as nothing had come to them from Tuscaloosa, they being from another section. Captain Lumsden sent for them and told them he would not insist on their going on parade, in that condition, but that if they would, he did not doubt, that it would result in getting them some clothing. They decided to go. So, when the parade was formed on Government Street, for General Maury's inspection, these men showed up in the front rank, and caught the general's eye. He rode up to Lumsden and asked: "Captain, what does that mean, those men in ranks, in that condition?"

"They have no clothing, Sir, but what they have on, and I have exhausted all means to obtain it, by requisition after requisition."

"Can't you think of some way, Captain?"

"If you will allow me to detail a man to go to Tuscaloosa, I do not doubt we can get all the clothes needed, in some way."

"All right, Captain, make the detail, I will endorse it, approved."

"Thank you, Sir, we will attend to it at once."

On return to camp, Captain Lumsden had orders written for the writer to proceed to Tuscaloosa on this business and started the papers up to headquarters in regular channel.

But about March 20th, we were sent over to Spanish Fort, on the Eastern shore of Mobile River or rather Spanish River as the eastern channel is called, by steamer. We were placed in charge of an angle, at about the centre of the fortified semi-circle that constituted the fort, armed with 4 six pounder field guns. They seemed like pop guns in comparison with the 12 pounder Napoleons, that we had handled so long.

We planted our front pretty thoroughly with mines, consisting of large shells buried with caps that would explode at the touch of a foot on a trigger, and we awaited the approach of the Federal force that had been landed below.

On March 26th, he arrived before us entrenched and we had several lively artillery duels while he was so doing.

By April 4th, he had in position 38 siege guns, including six 20 lb. rifles, 16 mortars and 37 field guns, when he opened fire at 5:00 a.m., and continued until 7:00 a.m., and so continued on April 5th, 6th and 7th. On April 8th, he had 53 siege guns in position, and 37 field guns. Closer and closer, came the parallels, each morning finding the Federal trenches closer than the day before, until any exposure of any part of the body, of either Yank or Confederate, would draw several bullets, men standing with rifles at shoulder beneath the head logs and finger on trigger, ready to fire at the least motion shown on opposite entrenchment.

We were furnished, each man with a rifle, as well as our artillery, and our shoulders got sore with the continued kick of the firing. We were moved once along the line nearer the river on the northern line of the fort.

Here, Lieutenant A. C. Hargrove, received the bullet that remained somewhere in his head during the balance of his life.

That afternoon the orders detailing the writer to go to Tuscaloosa came back from headquarters, they were handed to him, and he was ordered to start at once to get the boat that would leave that night. This ended the writer's personal experience in Lumsden's Battery. They evacuated with the garrison of the night of April and were transported over to Mobile, wading out into the bay to meet the relieving boat.

This practically ended the service of the command, which was transported by rail to Meridian and was part of the last organized command surrendered by General Dick Taylor with his department on the 4th day of May, 1865. There they went into service near Mobile, and after four years of active service in Alabama, Mississippi, Tennessee, Kentucky and Georgia, they were disbanded near the scene of their first service.

# Honor Role

LUMSDEN'S BATTERY, (LIGHT ARTILLERY)
C. S. A.
ORGANIZED NOV. 4, 1861

## (6) Officers

1. Charles L. Lumsden      Captain.
2. George W. Vaughn      Sr. First Lieut.
3. Harvey H. Cribbs      Jr. First Lieut.
4. Ebenezer H. Hargrove      Sr. Second Lieut.
5. Edward Tarrant      Jr. Second Lieut.
6. Joseph Porter Sykes      Cadet C. S. A.

## (14) Non-Commissioned Officers

1. George Little      Orderly Sergeant.
2. John Snow      Quartermaster Sergeant.
3. John A. Caldwell      Sergeant, First piece,
   later elected Lieut., and James
   R. Maxwell appointed in his place.
4. Wiley G. W. Hester      Sergeant, Second Piece.
5. Sam Hairston      Sergeant, Third Piece.
6. Horace Walpole Martin      Sergeant, Fourth Piece.
7. Andrew Coleman Hargrove      Sergeant, Fifth Piece.
8. James L. Miller      Sergeant, Sixth Piece.

## Corporals

1. J. Wick Brown      First Corporal
2. James Cardwell      Second Corporal
3. Alex T. Dearing      Third Corporal
4. William Hester      Fourth Corporal
5. Thomas Owen      Fifth Corporal
6. Seth Shepherd      Sixth Corporal

# Privates

1. Appling, Wm. B
2. Atkins
3. Austin, Thomas
4. Bates, William
5. Bartee, John P.
6. Barker, William
7. Barrett, Gideon
8. Barrett, Frank
9. Beatty, William
10. Baumeister, Joseph
11. Blackstock, Belson
12. Booth, James
13. Booth, David
14. Booth, Curtis
15. Braun, William
16. Brady, Dennis
17. Brooks, Wade
18. Browne, Newborne H
19. Bulger
20. Burleson
21. Conner
22. Cooper, William
23. Cosmer
24. Cox
25. Chancellor, John S.
26. Chancellor, M. H
27. Creel
28. Crocker
29. Cummins, St. John
30. Darden, Morgan, M.
31. Deason, Peter
32. Deason, Washington
33. Dehart
34. Delano, Sirenus
35. Donoho, Charles M.
94. Kahnweiler, Lewis
95. Kelly, Daniel
96. Kelly, Louis
97. Kilgore
98. King, Edward
99. Kuykendall
100. Lashley
101. Leslie
102. Lane
103. Lanneau, K. Palmer
104. Little, John, Jr.
105. Little, James
106. Lloyd, George
107. Maddox, John
108. Malone, William
109. Maner
110. Menning, John
111. Maxwell, James R.
112. Maxwell, Richard
113. Matthews
114. Maher, Dennis
115. Molette, John
116. Moore, Dr.
117. Morris, William
118. Milton
119. Moss
120. Moody, Joseph
121. Parish, James
122. Mason, Isaac
123. Nix, Ambrose
124. Nix, John
125. Parker, Foster
126. Pearce
127. Peoples, John
128. Peterson, H. C.

36. Donoho, Henry
37. Drake, John
38. Emerson, James
39. Evans, E. P.
40. Evans, John
41. Etheridge, Henry
42. Faucett, Thomas
43. Fiquet, Charles J.
44. Fleming, William
45. Foster, Robert S.
46. Foster, Robert Ware
47. Franks
48. Franks
49. Franks
50. Franks
51. Franks
52. Fulghem
53. Gaddy, R. M.
54. Garner, Abraham
55. Garner, John
56. Garner, Thomas
57. Goodwin, James
58. Goodwin, Wyche
59. Goodwin
60. Graham
61. Grayson, Preston
62. Guild, Walter
63. Gurley, Jacob
64. Hall, Joshua
65. Hall, John
66. Hall, Zach
67. Hamner, John
68. Haney, John W.
69. Hargrove, Arthur
70. Hargrove, Daniel
71. Hargrove, Rufus

129. Pollard, J. W.
130. Pool, Erwin P.
131. Post, Peter K.
132. Potts, Thomas W.
133. Papin
134. Ray, George
135. Raley
136. Renfro
137. Rosser, R. M.
138. Rosser, L. H.
139. Rosser, H. L.
140. Ryland, Joseph H.
141. Sadler
142. Sample, Joseph
143. Sartain
144. Savage, John
145. Scrivner, Sr., R.
146. Scrivner, Jr., R.
147. Scrivner, James
148. Sexton, Benjamen F.
149. Sexton, Horace H.
150. Shuttlesworth, R. F.
151. Shultz, David
152. Shultz, Thomas J.
153. Searcy, James T.
154. Sims, J. Marion
155. Staley, Charles
156. Shivers, J. Mc.
157. Sutton, Jack
158. Sykes, John
159. Smith, George W.
160. Tackett, William
161. Tarrant, John F.
162. Tarrant, William
163. Thompson, A. J.
164. Thompson, M. D.

72. Hargrove, Tenetus
73. Hester, William C.
74. Hester, Thomas J.
75. Higbee, V.
76. Highsaw, Nathaniel
77. Hildebrand
78. Hill, Dr.
79. Hogan, James
80. Holcomb, Thomas
81. Horton, John
82. Howard, Daniel
83. Howard, Charles B.
84. Hunter, Thomas
85. Hocutt
86. Hyche, Perry
87. Hyche, John
88. Hughes, Anthony
89. Jenkins, William
90. Johnson, William H.
91. Joncs, David
92. Jones, James T.
93. Jones, Lawrence

165. Thornton, Arthur
166. Thrower, J. T.
167. Tingle
168. Toole, George
169. Townsend
170. Trehorn
171. Vance, John
172. Vandiver, William
173. Walker, John
174. Walker, Robert G.
175. Waite
176. Watkins
177. Watkins, John
178. Weems, John
179. Wilborn, Thomas J.
180. Wilds
181. Winborn, D.
182. Williams
183. White
184. Winn, John
185. Woodruff, William
186. Wooley, B. F.

**Surgeons**: Marlowe, Nicholas, Perkins, McMichall and Jarratt.

## Summary

| | |
|---|---|
| Officers | 6 |
| Surgeons | 3 |
| Officers, Non-commissioned | 14 |
| Privates | 186 |
| Names not recalled | 16 |
| Total | 225 |

# Stonewall's Cannoneer

EXPERIENCES WITH THE ROCKBRIDGE ARTILLERY,
CONFEDERATE ARMY OF NORTHERN VIRGINIA,
DURING THE AMERICAN CIVIL WAR

EDWARD A. MOORE

*If you enjoyed this book you may also enjoy reading another Leonaur title concerning the artillerymen of the Confederacy and an extract follows for your enjoyment with our compliments.*

In less than five minutes one of Latimer's caissons was exploded, which called forth a lusty cheer from the enemy. In five minutes more a Federal caisson was blown up, which brought forth a louder cheer from us. In this action Latimer's batteries suffered fearfully, the Alleghany Roughs alone losing twenty-seven men killed and wounded. Only one or two were wounded in our battery, the proximity of Latimer's guns drawing the fire to them. Near the close of the engagement, Latimer, who was a graduate of the Virginia Military Institute, a mere youth in appearance, was killed.

The artillery contest was a small part of the afternoon's work. One of Johnson's brigades, after capturing breastworks and prisoners on Culp's Hill, pushed nearly to General Meade's headquarters. Rodes, usually so prompt, was occupying the town and failed to attack till late, and then with but two of his four brigades; but they charged over three lines of breastworks and captured several pieces of artillery, which had to be abandoned for want of support. Sickles's corps, having occupied the two "Round Tops" on the extreme left of the Federal line, advanced on Longstreet, and at four P.M.. the two lines met in the celebrated "Peach Orchard," and from that time until night fought furiously, the Federals being driven back to their original ground.

At the close of the second day the Confederates had gained ground on the right and left, and captured some artillery, but still nothing decisive. Another night passed, and the third and last day dawned on two anxious armies. Pickett, after a mysterious delay of twenty-four hours, arrived during the forenoon and became the left of Longstreet's corps. At twelve o'clock word was passed along our lines that when two signal-guns were heard, followed by heavy firing, to open vigorously with our guns. There was no mistaking when that time came, and we joined with the three hundred guns that made the firing. For an hour or more a crash and roar of artillery continued that rolled and reverberated above, and made the earth under us tremble. When it began there was great commotion among the enemy's batteries in our front, some of which limbered up and galloped along the crest of Cemetery Hill, but soon returned and renewed their fire on us.

So far they had failed to do our battery any serious harm, but now each volley of their shells came closer and closer. At this time my attention was attracted to the second piece, a few paces to our left, and I saw a shell plough into the ground under Lieutenant Brown's feet and explode. It tore a large hole, into which Brown sank, enveloped as he fell in smoke and dust. In an instant another shell burst at the trail of my gun, tearing the front half of Tom Williamson's shoe off, and wounding him sorely. A piece of it also broke James Ford's leg, besides cutting off the fore leg of Captain Graham's horse. Ford was holding the lead-horses of the limber, and, as they wheeled to run, their bridles were seized by Rader, a shell struck the horse nearest to him, and, exploding at the instant, killed all four of the lead-horses and stunned Rader. These same horses and this driver had very nearly a similar experience (though not so fatal) at Sharpsburg a year before, as already described. Sam Wilson, another member of our detachment, was also painfully wounded and knocked down by the same shell.

This artillery bombardment was the prelude to Pickett's charge, which took place on the opposite side of Cemetery Hill, and out of our view. Culp's Hill, since the early morning previous, had been enveloped in a veil of smoke from Johnson's muskets, which had scarcely had time to cool during the thirty-six hours.

The men of the Fourth Virginia Regiment had been gradually and steadily advancing from boulder to boulder, until they were almost under the enemy's fortifications along the crest of the ridge. To proceed farther was physically impossible, to retreat was almost certain death. So, of the College company alone, one of whom had already been killed and many wounded, sixteen, including Captain Strickler, were captured. To John McKee, of this company, a stalwart Irish Federal said as he reached out to pull him up over the breastworks, "Gimme your hand, Johnny Reb; you've give' us the bulliest fight of the war!"

Lieutenant "Cush" Jones determined to run the gauntlet for escape, and as he darted away the point of his scabbard struck a stone, and throwing it inverted above his head, lost out his handsome sword. Three bullets passed through his clothing in his flight, and the boulder behind which he next took refuge was peppered by others. Here, also, my former messmate, George Bedinger, now captain of a company in the Thirty-third Virginia Regiment, was killed, leading his "Greeks," as he called his men.

About nine o'clock that evening, and before we had moved from our position, I received a message, through Captain Graham, from some of the wounded of our company, to go to them at their field-hospital. Following the messenger, I found them in charge of our surgeon, Dr. Herndon, occupying a neat brick cottage a mile in the rear, from which the owners had fled, leaving a well-stocked larder, and from it we refreshed ourselves most gratefully. Toward midnight orders came to move. The ambulances were driven to the door and, after the wounded, some eight or ten in number, had been assisted into them, I added from the stores in the house a bucket of lard, a crock of butter, a jar of apple-butter, a ham, a middling of bacon, and a side of sole-leather. All for the wounded!

Feeling assured that we would not tarry much longer in Pennsylvania, and expecting to reach the battery before my services would be needed, I set out with the ambulances. We moved on until daylight and joined the wounded of the other batteries of our battalion, and soon after left, at a house by the wayside, a member of the Richmond Howitzers who was dying. Our course was along a by-road in the direction of Hagerstown. In the afternoon, after joining the wagon-train, I found "Joe," the coloured cook of my mess, in possession of a supernumerary battery-horse, which I appropriated and mounted. Our column now consisted of ambulances loaded with wounded men, wounded men on foot, cows, bulls, quartermasters, portable forges, surgeons, cooks, and camp-followers in general, all plodding gloomily along through the falling rain.

We arrived at the base of the mountain about five P. M. and began ascending by a narrow road, leading obliquely to the left. Before proceeding farther some description of the horse I was riding is appropriate, as he proved an important factor in my experiences before the night was over. He was the tallest horse I ever saw outside of a show, with a very short back and exceedingly long legs, which he handled peculiarly, going several gaits at one time. Many a cannoneer had sought rest on his back on the march, but none had ventured on so high a perch when going into battle. When half-way up the mountain we heard to our left oblique the distant mutter of a cannon, then in a few moments the sound was repeated, but we thought it was safely out of our course and felt correspondingly comfortable. At intervals the report of that gun was heard again and again. About dusk we reached the top of the mountain, after many, many halts, and the sound of that cannon became more emphatic.

After descending a few hundred yards there came from a bridle-path on our left, just as I passed it, three cavalry horses with empty saddles. This was rather ominous. The halts in the mixed column were now frequent, darkness having set in, and we had but little to say. That cannon had moved more to our front, and our road bore still more to where it was thundering. We were now almost at the foot of the mountain, and to the left, nearer our front, were scattering musket-shots. Our halts were still short and frequent, and in the deep shadow of the mountain it was pitch-dark. All of this time I had not a particle of confidence in my horse. I could not tell what was before me in the dense darkness, whether friend or foe, but suddenly, after pausing an instant, he dashed forward. For fifty or seventy-five yards every other sound was drowned by a roaring waterfall on my right; then, emerging from its noise, I was carried at a fearful rate close by dismounted men who were firing from behind trees along the roadside, the flashes of their guns, "whose speedy gleams the darkness swallowed," revealing me on my tall horse with his head up. He must see safety ahead, and I let him fly.

A hundred yards farther on our road joined the main pike at an acute angle, and entering it he swept on. Then, just behind me, a Federal cannon was discharged. The charge of canister tore through the brush on either side, and over and under me, and at the same instant my steed's hind leg gave way, and my heart sank with it. If struck at all, he immediately rallied and outran himself as well as his competitors. After getting out of the range of the firing and the shadow of the mountain, I saw indistinctly our cavalrymen along the side of the road, and we bantered each other as I passed.

Farther on, at a toll-gate, I heard the voice of Tom Williamson. His ambulance had broken down and he was being assisted toward the house. I drew rein, but thought, "How can I help him? This horse must be well-nigh done for," and rode on. Since reaching the foot of the mountain the way had been open and everything on it moving for life. But again the road was full, and approaching clatter, with the sharp reports of pistols, brought on another rush, and away we went—wagons, wounded men, negroes, forges, ambulances, cavalry—everything. This in time subsided and, feeling ashamed, I turned back to look after my wounded, my horse as reluctant as myself, and expecting every moment the sound of the coming foe. A sudden snort and the timid step of my nervous steed warned me of breakers ahead. Peering through the darkness I saw coming toward me, noiseless and swift as the wind, an object white as the driven snow. "What," I asked myself, "are ghosts abroad, and in such a place? Is Gettysburg giving up her dead so soon?" But, as the thing met me, a voice cried out, "Is that you, Ned? Is that you? Take me on your horse. Let me get in the saddle and you behind." For a moment I was dumb, and wished it wasn't I. The voice was the voice of Lieutenant Brown, the same whom I had seen undermined by the shell at Gettysburg, and who had not put a foot to the ground until now. Barefooted, bareheaded; nothing on but drawers and shirt—white as a shroud! The prospect that now confronted me instantly flashed through my mind. First, "Can this horse carry two?" Then I pictured myself with such a looking object in my embrace, and with nothing with which to conceal him. There were settlements ahead, daylight was approaching, and what a figure we would cut! It was too much for me, and I said, "No, get on behind," feeling that the spectre might retard the pursuing foe. But my tall horse solved the difficulty. Withdrawing my foot from the stirrup, Brown would put his in and try to climb up, when suddenly the horse would "swap ends," and down he'd go. Again he would try and almost make it, and the horse not wheeling quickly enough I would give him the hint with my "off" heel. My relief can be imagined when an ambulance arrived and took Brown in. I accompanied him for a short distance, then quickened my pace and overtook the train. Presently another clatter behind and the popping of pistols. Riding at my side was a horseman, and by the flash of his pistol I saw it pointing to the ground at our horses' feet.

Reaching the foot of a hill, my horse stumbled and fell as if to rise no more. I expected to be instantly trampled out of sight. I heard a groan, but not where the horse's head should have been. Resting my feet on the ground, thus relieving him of my weight, he got his head from under him and floundered forward, then to his feet and away. Farther on, a swift horse without a rider was dashing by me. I seized what I supposed to be his bridle-rein, but it proved to be the strap on the saddle-bow, and the pull I gave came near unhorsing me.

The pursuit continued no farther. Not having slept for two days and nights, I could not keep awake, and my game old horse, now wearied out, would stagger heedlessly against the wheels of moving wagons. Just at dawn of day, in company with a few horsemen of our battalion, I rode through the quiet streets of Hagerstown, thence seven miles to Williamsport.

The wounded of our battalion had all been captured. A few, however, were not carried off, but left until our army came up.

Some of the cooks, etc., escaped by dodging into the brush, but many a good horse and rider had been run down and taken. At Williamsport I exchanged horses with an infantryman while he was lying asleep on a porch, and had completed the transaction before he was sufficiently awake to remonstrate.

We were now entirely cut off from our army, and with what of the wagons, etc., that remained were at the mercy of the enemy, as the Potomac was swollen to a depth of twenty feet where I had waded a year before. Most of the horses had to be *swum over*, as there was little room in the ferry-boats for them. The river was so high that this was very dangerous, and only expert swimmers dared to undertake it. Twenty dollars was paid for swimming a horse over, and I saw numbers swept down by the current and landed hundreds of yards below, many on the side from which they had started. I crossed in a ferry-boat on my recently acquired horse, having left my faithful old charger, his head encased in mud to the tips of his ears, with mingled feelings of sadness and gratitude.

A great curiosity to understand this battle and battlefield induced me to visit it at the first opportunity, and in 1887, twenty-four years after it was fought, I, with Colonel Poague, gladly accepted an invitation from the survivors of Pickett's division to go with them to Gettysburg, whither they had been invited to meet the Philadelphia Brigade, as their guests, and go over the battlefield together. After our arrival there, in company with two officers of the Philadelphia Brigade, one of Pickett's men and an intelligent guide, I drove over the field. As a part of our entertainment we saw the Pickett men formed on the same ground and in the same order in which they had advanced to the charge. Farther on we saw the superb monuments, marking the location of the different Federal regiments, presenting the appearance of a vast cemetery. The position held by the Federals for defence was perfect. Its extent required the whole of the Confederate army present to occupy the one line they first adopted, with no troops to spare for flanking. Its shape, somewhat like a fish-hook, enabled the Federal army to reinforce promptly any part that was even threatened. Its terrain was such that the only ground sufficiently smooth for an enemy to advance on, that in front of its center, was exposed throughout, not only to missiles from its front, but could be raked from the heights on its left. And, in addition to all this, the whole face of the country, when the battle was fought, was closely intersected with post and rail and stone fences.

**LEONAUR**

# ALSO FROM LEONAUR
## AVAILABLE IN SOFTCOVER OR HARDCOVER WITH DUST JACKET

**A HISTORY OF THE FRENCH & INDIAN WAR** *by Arthur G. Bradley*—The Seven Years War as it was fought in the New World has always fascinated students of military history—here is the story of that confrontation.

**WASHINGTON'S EARLY CAMPAIGNS** *by James Hadden*—The French Post Expedition, Great Meadows and Braddock's Defeat—including Braddock's Orderly Books.

**BOUQUET & THE OHIO INDIAN WAR** *by Cyrus Cort & William Smith*—Two Accounts of the Campaigns of 1763-1764: Bouquet's Campaigns by Cyrus Cort & The History of Bouquet's Expeditions by William Smith.

**NARRATIVES OF THE FRENCH & INDIAN WAR: 2** *by David Holden, Samuel Jenks, Lemuel Lyon, Mary Cochrane Rogers & Henry T. Blake*—Contains The Diary of Sergeant David Holden, Captain Samuel Jenks' Journal, The Journal of Lemuel Lyon, Journal of a French Officer at the Siege of Quebec, A Battle Fought on Snowshoes & The Battle of Lake George.

**NARRATIVES OF THE FRENCH & INDIAN WAR** *by Brown, Eastburn, Hawks & Putnam*—Ranger Brown's Narrative, The Adventures of Robert Eastburn, The Journal of Rufus Putnam—Provincial Infantry & Orderly Book and Journal of Major John Hawks on the Ticonderoga-Crown Point Campaign.

**THE 7TH (QUEEN'S OWN) HUSSARS: Volume 1—1688-1792** *by C. R. B. Barrett*—As Dragoons During the Flanders Campaign, War of the Austrian Succession and the Seven Years War.

**INDIA'S FREE LANCES** *by H. G. Keene*—European Mercenary Commanders in Hindustan 1770-1820.

**THE BENGAL EUROPEAN REGIMENT** *by P. R. Innes*—An Elite Regiment of the Honourable East India Company 1756-1858.

**MUSKET & TOMAHAWK** *by Francis Parkman*—A Military History of the French & Indian War, 1753-1760.

**THE BLACK WATCH AT TICONDEROGA** *by Frederick B. Richards*—Campaigns in the French & Indian War.

**QUEEN'S RANGERS** *by Frederick B. Richards*—John Simcoe and his Rangers During the Revolutionary War for America.

LEONAUR

# ALSO FROM LEONAUR
## AVAILABLE IN SOFTCOVER OR HARDCOVER WITH DUST JACKET

**JOURNALS OF ROBERT ROGERS OF THE RANGERS** *by Robert Rogers*—The exploits of Rogers & the Rangers in his own words during 1755-1761 in the French & Indian War.

**GALLOPING GUNS** *by James Young*—The Experiences of an Officer of the Bengal Horse Artillery During the Second Maratha War 1804-1805.

**GORDON** *by Demetrius Charles Boulger*—The Career of Gordon of Khartoum.

**THE BATTLE OF NEW ORLEANS** *by Zachary F. Smith*—The final major engagement of the War of 1812.

**THE TWO WARS OF MRS DUBERLY** *by Frances Isabella Duberly*—An Intrepid Victorian Lady's Experience of the Crimea and Indian Mutiny.

**WITH THE GUARDS' BRIGADE DURING THE BOER WAR** *by Edward P. Lowry*—On Campaign from Bloemfontein to Koomati Poort and Back.

**THE REBELLIOUS DUCHESS** *by Paul F. S. Dermoncourt*—The Adventures of the Duchess of Berri and Her Attempt to Overthrow French Monarchy.

**MEN OF THE MUTINY** *by John Tulloch Nash & Henry Metcalfe*—Two Accounts of the Great Indian Mutiny of 1857: Fighting with the Bengal Yeomanry Cavalry & Private Metcalfe at Lucknow.

**CAMPAIGN IN THE CRIMEA** *by George Shuldham Peard*—The Recollections of an Officer of the 20th Regiment of Foot.

**WITHIN SEBASTOPOL** *by K. Hodasevich*—A Narrative of the Campaign in the Crimea, and of the Events of the Siege.

**WITH THE CAVALRY TO AFGHANISTAN** *by William Taylor*—The Experiences of a Trooper of H. M. 4th Light Dragoons During the First Afghan War.

**THE CAWNPORE MAN** *by Mowbray Thompson*—A First Hand Account of the Siege and Massacre During the Indian Mutiny By One of Four Survivors.

**BRIGADE COMMANDER: AFGHANISTAN** *by Henry Brooke*—The Journal of the Commander of the 2nd Infantry Brigade, Kandahar Field Force During the Second Afghan War.

**BANCROFT OF THE BENGAL HORSE ARTILLERY** *by N. W. Bancroft*—An Account of the First Sikh War 1845-1846.

**LEONAUR**

# ALSO FROM LEONAUR
## AVAILABLE IN SOFTCOVER OR HARDCOVER WITH DUST JACKET

**ZULU:1879** *by D.C.F. Moodie & the Leonaur Editors*—The Anglo-Zulu War of 1879 from contemporary sources: First Hand Accounts, Interviews, Dispatches, Official Documents & Newspaper Reports.

**THE RED DRAGOON** *by W.J. Adams*—With the 7th Dragoon Guards in the Cape of Good Hope against the Boers & the Kaffir tribes during the 'war of the axe' 1843-48'.

**THE RECOLLECTIONS OF SKINNER OF SKINNER'S HORSE** *by James Skinner*—James Skinner and his 'Yellow Boys' Irregular cavalry in the wars of India between the British, Mahratta, Rajput, Mogul, Sikh & Pindarree Forces.

**A CAVALRY OFFICER DURING THE SEPOY REVOLT** *by A. R. D. Mackenzie*—Experiences with the 3rd Bengal Light Cavalry, the Guides and Sikh Irregular Cavalry from the outbreak to Delhi and Lucknow.

**A NORFOLK SOLDIER IN THE FIRST SIKH WAR** *by J W Baldwin*—Experiences of a private of H.M. 9th Regiment of Foot in the battles for the Punjab, India 1845-6.

**TOMMY ATKINS' WAR STORIES: 14 FIRST HAND ACCOUNTS**—Fourteen first hand accounts from the ranks of the British Army during Queen Victoria's Empire.

**THE WATERLOO LETTERS** *by H. T. Siborne*—Accounts of the Battle by British Officers for its Foremost Historian.

**NEY: GENERAL OF CAVALRY VOLUME 1—1769-1799** *by Antoine Bulos*—The Early Career of a Marshal of the First Empire.

**NEY: MARSHAL OF FRANCE VOLUME 2—1799-1805** *by Antoine Bulos*—The Early Career of a Marshal of the First Empire.

**AIDE-DE-CAMP TO NAPOLEON** *by Philippe-Paul de Ségur*—For anyone interested in the Napoleonic Wars this book, written by one who was intimate with the strategies and machinations of the Emperor, will be essential reading.

**TWILIGHT OF EMPIRE** *by Sir Thomas Ussher & Sir George Cockburn*—Two accounts of Napoleon's Journeys in Exile to Elba and St. Helena: Narrative of Events by Sir Thomas Ussher & Napoleon's Last Voyage: Extract of a diary by Sir George Cockburn.

**PRIVATE WHEELER** *by William Wheeler*—The letters of a soldier of the 51st Light Infantry during the Peninsular War & at Waterloo.

LEONAUR

# ALSO FROM LEONAUR
## AVAILABLE IN SOFTCOVER OR HARDCOVER WITH DUST JACKET

**OMPTEDA OF THE KING'S GERMAN LEGION** *by Christian von Ompteda*—A Hanoverian Officer on Campaign Against Napoleon.

**LIEUTENANT SIMMONS OF THE 95TH (RIFLES)** *by George Simmons*—Recollections of the Peninsula, South of France & Waterloo Campaigns of the Napoleonic Wars.

**A HORSEMAN FOR THE EMPEROR** *by Jean Baptiste Gazzola*—A Cavalryman of Napoleon's Army on Campaign Throughout the Napoleonic Wars.

**SERGEANT LAWRENCE** *by William Lawrence*—With the 40th Regt. of Foot in South America, the Peninsular War & at Waterloo.

**CAMPAIGNS WITH THE FIELD TRAIN** *by Richard D. Henegan*—Experiences of a British Officer During the Peninsula and Waterloo Campaigns of the Napoleonic Wars.

**CAVALRY SURGEON** *by S. D. Broughton*—On Campaign Against Napoleon in the Peninsula & South of France During the Napoleonic Wars 1812-1814.

**MEN OF THE RIFLES** *by Thomas Knight, Henry Curling & Jonathan Leach*—The Reminiscences of Thomas Knight of the 95th (Rifles) by Thomas Knight, Henry Curling's Anecdotes by Henry Curling & The Field Services of the Rifle Brigade from its Formation to Waterloo by Jonathan Leach.

**THE ULM CAMPAIGN 1805** *by F. N. Maude*—Napoleon and the Defeat of the Austrian Army During the 'War of the Third Coalition'.

**SOLDIERING WITH THE 'DIVISION'** *by Thomas Garrety*—The Military Experiences of an Infantryman of the 43rd Regiment During the Napoleonic Wars.

**SERGEANT MORRIS OF THE 73RD FOOT** *by Thomas Morris*—The Experiences of a British Infantryman During the Napoleonic Wars-Including Campaigns in Germany and at Waterloo.

**A VOICE FROM WATERLOO** *by Edward Cotton*—The Personal Experiences of a British Cavalryman Who Became a Battlefield Guide and Authority on the Campaign of 1815.

**NAPOLEON AND HIS MARSHALS** *by J. T. Headley*—The Men of the First Empire.

LEONAUR

# ALSO FROM LEONAUR
## AVAILABLE IN SOFTCOVER OR HARDCOVER WITH DUST JACKET

**THE LIFE OF THE REAL BRIGADIER GERARD VOLUME 1—THE YOUNG HUSSAR 1782-1807** *by Jean-Baptiste De Marbot*—A French Cavalryman Of the Napoleonic Wars at Marengo, Austerlitz, Jena, Eylau & Friedland.

**THE LIFE OF THE REAL BRIGADIER GERARD VOLUME 2—IMPERIAL AIDE-DE-CAMP 1807-1811** *by Jean-Baptiste De Marbot*—A French Cavalryman of the Napoleonic Wars at Saragossa, Landshut, Eckmuhl, Ratisbon, Aspern-Essling, Wagram, Busaco & Torres Vedras.

**THE LIFE OF THE REAL BRIGADIER GERARD VOLUME 3—COLONEL OF CHASSEURS 1811-1815** *by Jean-Baptiste De Marbot*—A French Cavalryman in the retreat from Moscow, Lutzen, Bautzen, Katzbach, Leipzig, Hanau & Waterloo.

**THE INDIAN WAR OF 1864** *by Eugene Ware*—The Experiences of a Young Officer of the 7th Iowa Cavalry on the Western Frontier During the Civil War.

**THE MARCH OF DESTINY** *by Charles E. Young & V. Devinny*—Dangers of the Trail in 1865 by Charles E. Young & The Story of a Pioneer by V. Devinny, two Accounts of Early Emigrants to Colorado.

**CROSSING THE PLAINS** *by William Audley Maxwell*—A First Hand Narrative of the Early Pioneer Trail to California in 1857.

**CHIEF OF SCOUTS** *by William F. Drannan*—A Pilot to Emigrant and Government Trains, Across the Plains of the Western Frontier.

**THIRTY-ONE YEARS ON THE PLAINS AND IN THE MOUNTAINS** *by William F. Drannan*—William Drannan was born to be a pioneer, hunter, trapper and wagon train guide during the momentous days of the Great American West.

**THE INDIAN WARS VOLUNTEER** *by William Thompson*—Recollections of the Conflict Against the Snakes, Shoshone, Bannocks, Modocs and Other Native Tribes of the American North West.

**THE 4TH TENNESSEE CAVALRY** *by George B. Guild*—The Services of Smith's Regiment of Confederate Cavalry by One of its Officers.

**COLONEL WORTHINGTON'S SHILOH** *by T. Worthington*—The Tennessee Campaign, 1862, by an Officer of the Ohio Volunteers.

**FOUR YEARS IN THE SADDLE** *by W. L. Curry*—The History of the First Regiment Ohio Volunteer Cavalry in the American Civil War.

LEONAUR

# ALSO FROM LEONAUR
## AVAILABLE IN SOFTCOVER OR HARDCOVER WITH DUST JACKET

**LIFE IN THE ARMY OF NORTHERN VIRGINIA** *by Carlton McCarthy*— The Observations of a Confederate Artilleryman of Cutshaw's Battalion During the American Civil War 1861-1865.

**HISTORY OF THE CAVALRY OF THE ARMY OF THE POTOMAC** *by Charles D. Rhodes*—Including Pope's Army of Virginia and the Cavalry Operations in West Virginia During the American Civil War.

**CAMP-FIRE AND COTTON-FIELD** *by Thomas W. Knox*—A New York Herald Correspondent's View of the American Civil War.

**SERGEANT STILLWELL** *by Leander Stillwell* —The Experiences of a Union Army Soldier of the 61st Illinois Infantry During the American Civil War.

**STONEWALL'S CANNONEER** *by Edward A. Moore*—Experiences with the Rockbridge Artillery, Confederate Army of Northern Virginia, During the American Civil War.

**THE SIXTH CORPS** *by George Stevens*—The Army of the Potomac, Union Army, During the American Civil War.

**THE RAILROAD RAIDERS** *by William Pittenger*—An Ohio Volunteers Recollections of the Andrews Raid to Disrupt the Confederate Railroad in Georgia During the American Civil War.

**CITIZEN SOLDIER** *by John Beatty*—An Account of the American Civil War by a Union Infantry Officer of Ohio Volunteers Who Became a Brigadier General.

**COX: PERSONAL RECOLLECTIONS OF THE CIVIL WAR--VOLUME 1** *by Jacob Dolson Cox*—West Virginia, Kanawha Valley, Gauley Bridge, Cotton Mountain, South Mountain, Antietam, the Morgan Raid & the East Tennessee Campaign.

**COX: PERSONAL RECOLLECTIONS OF THE CIVIL WAR--VOLUME 2** *by Jacob Dolson Cox*—Siege of Knoxville, East Tennessee, Atlanta Campaign, the Nashville Campaign & the North Carolina Campaign.

**KERSHAW'S BRIGADE VOLUME 1** *by D. Augustus Dickert*—Manassas, Seven Pines, Sharpsburg (Antietam), Fredricksburg, Chancellorsville, Gettysburg, Chickamauga, Chattanooga, Fort Sanders & Bean Station.

**KERSHAW'S BRIGADE VOLUME 2** *by D. Augustus Dickert*—At the wilderness, Cold Harbour, Petersburg, The Shenandoah Valley and Cedar Creek..

AVAILABLE ONLINE AT **www.leonaur.com**
AND FROM ALL GOOD BOOK STORES                    07/09

**LEONAUR**

# ALSO FROM LEONAUR

## AVAILABLE IN SOFTCOVER OR HARDCOVER WITH DUST JACKET

**IRON TIMES WITH THE GUARDS** *by An O. E. (G. P. A. Fildes)*—The Experiences of an Officer of the Coldstream Guards on the Western Front During the First World War.

**THE GREAT WAR IN THE MIDDLE EAST: 1** *by W. T. Massey*—The Desert Campaigns & How Jerusalem Was Won---two classic accounts in one volume.

**THE GREAT WAR IN THE MIDDLE EAST: 2** *by W. T. Massey*—Allenby's Final Triumph.

**SMITH-DORRIEN** *by Horace Smith-Dorrien*—Isandlwhana to the Great War.

**1914** *by Sir John French*—The Early Campaigns of the Great War by the British Commander.

**GRENADIER** *by E. R. M. Fryer*—The Recollections of an Officer of the Grenadier Guards throughout the Great War on the Western Front.

**BATTLE, CAPTURE & ESCAPE** *by George Pearson*—The Experiences of a Canadian Light Infantryman During the Great War.

**DIGGERS AT WAR** *by R. Hugh Knyvett & G. P. Cuttriss*—"Over There" With the Australians by R. Hugh Knyvett and Over the Top With the Third Australian Division by G. P. Cuttriss. Accounts of Australians During the Great War in the Middle East, at Gallipoli and on the Western Front.

**HEAVY FIGHTING BEFORE US** *by George Brenton Laurie*—The Letters of an Officer of the Royal Irish Rifles on the Western Front During the Great War.

**THE CAMELIERS** *by Oliver Hogue*—A Classic Account of the Australians of the Imperial Camel Corps During the First World War in the Middle East.

**RED DUST** *by Donald Black*—A Classic Account of Australian Light Horsemen in Palestine During the First World War.

**THE LEAN, BROWN MEN** *by Angus Buchanan*—Experiences in East Africa During the Great War with the 25th Royal Fusiliers—the Legion of Frontiersmen.

**THE NIGERIAN REGIMENT IN EAST AFRICA** *by W. D. Downes*—On Campaign During the Great War 1916-1918.

**THE 'DIE-HARDS' IN SIBERIA** *by John Ward*—With the Middlesex Regiment Against the Bolsheviks 1918-19.

www.ingramcontent.com/pod-product-compliance
Lightning Source LLC
Chambersburg PA
CBHW020506100426
42813CB00030B/3142/J